the HOW-TO BOOK

LOVING GOD, LOVING OTHERS

the HOW-TO BOOK

LOVING GOD, LOVING OTHERS

Edited by
Jan P. Dennis

GOOD NEWS PUBLISHERS
WESTCHESTER, ILLINOIS

THE HOW-TO BOOK:
Loving God, Loving Others

Copyright © 1976 Good News Publishers,
Westchester, Illinois 60153.
All rights reserved.
Printed in the United States of America

Cover Design: Wayne Hanna

Library of Congress Catalog Number 76-17671
ISBN 0-89107-145-8

CONTENTS

Preface 7

PART I: LOVING GOD

Introduction 11
1. How to Meet God
   C. S. Lewis 13
2. How to Begin the Christian Life
   George Sweeting 19
3. How to Be the Friend of God
   Frederic Hood 27
4. How to Know God
   J. I. Packer 37
5. How to Read the Bible
   Claude H. Thompson 49
6. How to Take Hold of the Bible
   Don Fields 55
7. How to Experience the Transforming Power
   of the Holy Spirit
   J. Oswald Sanders 59

PART II: LOVING OTHERS

Introduction 69
8. How to Live in a Family and Like It
   Edith Schaeffer 73
9. How to Be a Wise Steward of God's Gifts
   Charles C. Ryrie 95

10. How to Face the Death of a Loved One
    Elisabeth Elliot 107
11. How to Overcome the Time Trap
    Bob Sheffield 115
12. How to Act Like a Christian
    L. Nelson Bell 119
13. How to Get Along with Other Christians
    Robert Webber 123
14. How to Deepen Church Life Through Small Groups
    Howard A. Snyder 131
15. How to Equip the Saints for God's Service
    Otis E. Young 139

About the Authors 151

PREFACE

The Christian life has often been compared to a pilgrimage or journey. In 11 different places in his letters to young churches, St. Paul speaks of the Christian's walk. Similarly, classics of Christian literature, like John Bunyan's *Pilgrim's Progress* and J. R. R. Tolkien's *Lord of the Rings*, have effectively used this image to illuminate the process of growth toward union with God through Jesus Christ, the Christian's goal in life.

In order to walk worthy of this high calling, Christians need a road map. Though we have been given one in the Holy Scriptures, no one can stay on the path without regular, disciplined reading of the only infallible guide we have to faith and practice, the inspired work of God. This point is made over and over again in chapters that follow.

Using the Bible both as guide and source of energy, this book is intended as a light to illumine the Christian way. Would-be pilgrims are given their first instructions on how to meet God by C. S. Lewis, a man whose own encounter with Light is beautifully told in his autobiography, *Surprised by Joy*. The rest of the first part of the book suggests ways of deepening one's relationship with God.

The second part of the book offers creative approaches towards establishing healthy relationships with fellow brothers and sisters in Christ—whether they be members of one's family (as in Edith Schaeffer's delightful chapter), or members of a different denomination (as in Robert Webber's provocative essay).

No single book can adequately cover all aspects of Christian living. But here is a collection of essays by prominent Christian writers known for their practical, straightforward answers to the question, "How does one live the Christian life?"   JAN P. DENNIS

PART I:

LOVING GOD

INTRODUCTION

During Jesus Christ's earthly ministry, He was asked which commandment was the greatest. He replied, "You shall love the Lord your God with all your heart, and with all your soul, and with all your mind. This is the great and first commandment" (Matthew 22:37, 38).

Part I of this book is a basic survey of how to fulfill the great commandment.

We can't love someone we don't know, and we can't get to know someone we haven't met. Therefore, before we can love God we must first meet Him. How do we go about this? In "How To Meet God" C. S. Lewis says it's not so much a matter of us searching for God as letting Him find us. All that's required on our part is to recognize His indefatigable efforts to make us aware of His presence—something we can scarcely avoid if we spend any time at all in solitude or silence, looking at nature, or reading the Bible.

Meeting (or being met by) God is only the first step in beginning to love God. In "How to Begin the Christian Life" George Sweeting clearly and simply explains what we need to believe about God and His Son, Jesus Christ, in order to begin to truly love Him. We must acknowledge that we have done wrong in God's eyes, that we have failed, that we are sinners. Then we must believe that Jesus Christ gave up His life, sacrificed Himself on our behalf, so that we would not have to endure eternal separation from God—the just penalty for our sin. By confessing our unworthiness and putting our faith in Jesus Christ, we are in a position to become friends with God. What a privilege—and what a responsibility! We are called to do no less than "present [our] bodies a living sacrifice, holy, acceptable unto God, which is [our] reasonable service" (Romans 12:1). Frederic Hood works out some basic ways of meeting this obligation—and the benefits that will be ours if we do. First and foremost, this means spending time with God. If we love someone, we will want to give up our time to be with him. The best way "to be with" God is through prayer. Hood's discourse on prayer is remarkable for its clarity and simplicity.

As we grow in the knowledge and love of God we'll likely reach a point where we desire to know Him more intimately than any person or object of our experience. J. I. Packer in "How To Know God" says that this desire on our part is a response to and recognition of God's great love towards us. Packer, along with Claude Thompson in "How to Read the Bible" and Don Fields in "How to Take Hold of the Bible," emphasizes in-depth Scripture reading as indispensible to knowing God. These three chapters are full of helpful suggestions on how to make Bible reading more meaningful.

The last chapter in Part I, "How To Experience the Transforming Power of the Holy Spirit," deals with an area of loving God that has only recently received its rightful attention, after years of neglect by the Church. Here J. Oswald Sanders emphasizes the need for Christians to actively cooperate with their renewed wills in the sanctifying activity of the Holy Spirit. Passivity is not enough. To love God fully, we must act in accordance with the efforts of the Holy Spirit to bring us into "mature manhood, to the measure of the stature of the fulness of Christ" (Ephesians 4:13).

Part I then, "Loving God," focuses on the basic Christian response—the initial and continual response that gives meaning to all other activity. In Part II we shall examine what should be the natural consequence of "Loving God"— "Loving Others."

J. P. D.

CHAPTER 1

HOW TO MEET GOD
C. S. LEWIS

THE RUSSIANS HAVE reported (rather triumphantly) that they did not find God in outer space. On the other hand, a good many people in different times and countries have claimed to have found God, or been found by God, here on earth.

The conclusion some have drawn from the Russian data is that God does not exist. As a corollary, those who think they have met Him on earth are suffering from a delusion. But other conclusions might be drawn:

1. We have not yet gone far enough in space. There had been ships on the Atlantic for a long time before America was discovered.

2. God does exist but is confined to this planet.

3. The Russians did find God in space without knowing it, because they lacked the requisite apparatus for detecting Him.

4. God does exist but is not an object either located in a particular part of space or diffused (as we once thought "ether" was) throughout space.

The first two conclusions do not interest me. The sort of religion for which they could be a defense would be a religion for savages, belief in a local deity who can be contained in a particular temple, island or grove. That, in fact, seems to be the sort of religion about which the Russians—or some Russians, and a good many people in the West—are being irreligious. It is not in the least disquieting that astronauts have not discovered a god of that sort. The really disquieting thing would be if they had.

The third and fourth conclusions are the ones for my money.

Looking for God (or heaven) by exploring space is like seeing all Shakespeare's plays in the hope that you will find Shakespeare as one of the characters, or Stratford as one of the places. Shakespeare is in one sense present at every moment in every play. But he is never present in the same way as Falstaff or Lady Macbeth. Nor is he diffused through the play like a gas.

If there were an idiot who thought plays existed on their own, without an author (not to mention actors, producer, manager, stagehands and what not), our belief in Shakespeare would not be much affected by his saying, quite truly, that he had studied all the plays and never found Shakespeare in them.

The rest of us, in varying degrees according to our perceptiveness, "found Shakespeare" in the plays. But it is a quite different sort of "finding" from anything our poor friend has in mind.

Even he has in reality been in some way affected by Shakespeare, but without knowing it. He lacked the necessary apparatus for detecting Shakespeare.

Now of course this is only an analogy. I am not suggesting at all that the existence of God is as easily established as the existence of Shakespeare. My point is that, if God does exist, He is related to the universe more as an author is related to a play than as one object in the universe is related to another.

If God created the universe, He created spacetime, which is to the universe as the meter is to a poem or the key is to music. To look for Him as one item within the framework which He Himself invented is nonsensical.

If God—such a God as any adult religion believes in—exists, mere movement in space will never bring you any nearer to Him or any farther from Him than you are at this very moment. You can neither reach Him nor avoid Him by traveling to Alpha Centauri or even to other galaxies. A fish is no more and no less in the sea after it has swum a thousand miles than it was when it set out.

HOW TO AVOID GOD

How, then, it may be asked, can we either reach or avoid God?

The avoiding, in many times and places, has proved so difficult that a very large part of the human race has failed to achieve it. But in our own time and place it is extremely easy. Avoid silence, avoid solitude, avoid any train of thought that leads off the beaten track. Concentrate on money, sex, status, health and (above all) on your own grievances. Keep the radio on. Live in a crowd. Use plenty of sedation. If you must read books, select them very carefully. But you'd be safer to stick to the papers. You'll find the advertisements helpful; especially those with a sexy or a snobbish appeal.

HOW TO FIND GOD

About the reaching, I am a far less reliable guide. That is because I never had the experience of looking for God. It was the other way round: He was the hunter (or so it seemed to me) and I was the deer. He stalked me like a redskin, took unerring aim, and fired. And I am very thankful that that is how the first (conscious) meeting occurred. It forearms one against subsequent fears that the whole thing was only wish fulfillment. Something one didn't wish for can hardly be that.

But it is significant that this long-evaded encounter happened at a time when I was making a serious effort to obey my conscience. No doubt it was far less serious than I supposed, but it was the most serious effort I had made for a long time.

WHAT ABOUT CHRIST?

And this is especially confirmed by my own religion, which is Christianity. When I said a while ago that it was nonsensical to look for God as one item within His own work, the universe, some readers may have protested. They wanted to say, "But surely, according to Christianity, that is just what did once happen? Surely the central doctrine is that God became man and walked about among other men in Palestine? If that is not appearing as an item in His own work, what is it?"

The objection is much to the point. To meet it, I must readjust my old analogy of the play. One might imagine a play in which the dramatist introduced himself as a character into his own play and was pelted off the stage as an impudent impostor by the other characters. It might be rather a good play; if I had any talent for the theater, I'd try my hand at writing it. But since as far as I know such a play doesn't exist, we had better change to a narrative work; a story into which the author puts himself as one of the characters.

We have a real instance of this in Dante's *Divine Comedy*. Dante is (1) the muse outside the poem who is inventing the whole thing, and (2) a character inside the poem whom the other characters meet and with whom they hold conversations. Where the analogy breaks down is that everything the poem contains is merely imaginary in that the characters have no free will. They (the characters) can say to Dante only what Dante (the poet) has decided to put into their mouths. I do not think we humans are related to God in that way. I think God can make things which not only *seem* to have a partially independent life (like a poet's or novelist's characters), but really have it. But the analogy furnishes a crude model of the incarnation in two respects: (1) Dante the poet and Dante the character are in a sense one, but in another sense two. This is a faint and far-off suggestion of what theologians mean by the "union of the two natures" (divine and human) in Christ. (2) The other people in the poem meet and see and hear Dante; but they have not even the faintest suspicion that he is making the whole world in which they exist and has a life of his own, outside it, independent of it.

It is the second point which is most relevant. The Christian story is that Christ was perceived to be God by very few people indeed; perhaps, for a time only by Peter, who would also and for the same reason have found God in space. For Christ said to Peter, "Flesh and blood have not taught you this." The methods of science do not discover facts of that order.

Indeed the expectation of finding God by astronautics would be very like trying to verify or falsify the divinity of Christ by taking specimens of His blood or dissecting Him. And in their own way they did both. But they were no wiser than before. What is required is a certain faculty of recognition.

If you do not at all know God, of course you will not recognize Him, either in Jesus or in outer space.

Space travel really has nothing to do with the matter. To some, God is discoverable everywhere; to others, nowhere. Those who do not find Him on earth are unlikely to find Him in space. (Hang it all, we're in space already; every year we make a huge circular tour in space.) But send a saint up in a spaceship and he'll find God in space as he found God on earth. Much depends on the seeing eye.

CHAPTER 2

HOW TO BEGIN THE CHRISTIAN LIFE

GEORGE SWEETING

For other foundation can no man lay than that is laid, which is Jesus Christ.

I CORINTHIANS 3:11

When by the Spirit of God, I understood these words, "The just shall live by faith," I felt born again like a new man: I entered through the open doors into the very Paradise of God!

MARTIN LUTHER

YOU, MY FRIEND, have taken a life-changing step. You have decided to begin a new life. God has become your heavenly Father and you are now His child; a wonderful eternal relationship has begun. It is really a brand-new beginning. In the words of Jesus, you have been "born again."

Possibly you feel very helpless to explain what has taken place. A new sense of freedom is yours. You are something like a happy child let loose in a big park. Practically everything is touched with divine newness and it is

---

From *How to Begin the Christian Life,* copyright 1976, by Moody Bible Institute, used by permission.

delicious. Do not be perplexed by what you have experienced, for this is wonderfully normal and right. The apostle Paul puts it this way, "Therefore if any man be in Christ, he is a new creature: old things are passed away; behold, all things are become new" (II Corinthians 5:17). When you receive Jesus Christ, you become a brand-new person.

WHAT YOU HAVE DONE
1. You have acknowledged your need as a sinner.

What is this decision that you have made? You have acknowledged that you were wrong and God is right. You have agreed with God that you yourself are spiritually bankrupt. You have told the Lord of the poverty of your soul. Earnestly you have prayed, "God be merciful to me a sinner" (Luke 18:13). Your first step was to acknowledge your need as a sinner.

Dead and *lost* are the two Bible words used to describe your past life. Dead things cannot grow. You do not grow *into* grace; you grow once you are in it. Nothing is so completely helpless as that which is dead; and as far as God is concerned, all people through natural birth are spiritually dead. The Bible describes your spiritual transformation this way: "And you hath he quickened, who were dead in trespasses and sins" (Ephesians 2:1). Your life has been changed from a dead to a living state in Christ. God has touched your life and imparted divine life—His life—eternal life. This decision is really a death-breaking, earth-shaking, heaven-awakening decision.

Lost is a descriptive word. The Bible states, "For the Son of man is come to seek and to save that which was lost" (Luke 19:10). Without Christ we are lost like sheep without a shepherd, helpless, hopeless, and defenseless. Lost, like the prodigal son, separated, destitute, and disgraced. By your decision you have been changed from a lost to a saved condition, changed from an enemy of God to a friend of God, changed from a stranger to a child of God. Your salvation is revolutionary.

Seneca, the philosopher, said, "We have all sinned, some more, some less."

Coleridge, the great thinker, confessed, "I am a fallen creature."

T. S. Eliot's character, Cecilia Copplestone, talks about her "awareness of solitude" and "a sense of sin."

The Chinese speak of "two good men: one dead, the other unborn."

The Bible plainly says, "For all have sinned, and come short of the glory of God" (Romans 3:23).

2. *You have acknowledged Jesus Christ as your Saviour.*

The Lord Jesus Christ came into this world to meet our basic need. Christ was born to die. "This is a faithful saying, and worthy of all acceptation, that Christ Jesus came into the world to save sinners" (I Timothy 1:15). This purpose was accomplished when He died on the cross. Repeatedly He told His disciples of His coming death. On the night of His betrayal by Judas, He broke bread with His disciples. Plainly He explained to them the purpose of the cross. "For this is my blood of the new testament, which is shed for many for the remission of sins" (Matthew 26:28). Paul simply and clearly wrote, "For he [God] hath made him to be sin for us, who knew no sin" (II Corinthians 5:21).

Isaiah prophetically penned, "But he was wounded for our transgressions, he was bruised for our iniquities: the chastisement of our peace was upon him; and with his stripes we are healed" (Isaiah 53:5).

Our basic need is the forgiveness of sin. God's provision for our need is found in the death of Jesus Christ. Jesus Christ, the sinless Son, fully and completely bore the sins of the world. He took upon Himself our sin. The Gospel is the Good News of what God has done through Christ to forgive our sins.

Recognizing Christ as God's answer, that He died in your

place, you have come asking for forgiveness of all your sins. "For Christ also hath once suffered for sins, the just for the unjust, that he might bring us to God" (I Peter 3:18). In a definite act of faith, you have pledged your allegiance to Christ. At that moment, Jesus became your Saviour, and God forgave your sins.

The word *confess* is an interesting word. It simply means to speak the same thing. It means to agree or acknowledge. You have first acknowledged your need as a sinner, but you have secondly acknowledged Jesus Christ as your personal Saviour. What have you done? "Thou hast believed" (John 20:29).

3. *You are now beginning to acknowledge Jesus Christ before others*

You may ask, "Do I have to publicly confess Christ?"

I must answer, "Yes, Jesus Christ requests a public confession." And I might add, "How can you help it!"

Jesus plainly said, "Whosoever therefore shall confess me before men, him will I confess also before my Father which is in heaven" (Matthew 10:32). If you have sincerely trusted Christ, you will have to tell someone about it. This new life will be obvious, for ' out of the abundance of the heart the mouth speaketh" (Matthew 12:34).

Some new Christians try to be "secret" believers, but this is unwise and wrong. Just imagine Dr. Jonas Salk keeping his polio vaccine a secret! This would have been criminal. So, too, a knowledge of God's salvation places us in debt to the whole world.

Both Nicodemus and Joseph of Arimathea tried to be secret disciples. It took the death of Christ to bring them to the place of openly begging the body of Jesus from Pilate. The Scripture record is clear: "And after this Joseph of Arimathea, being a disciple of Jesus, but secretly for fear of the Jews, besought Pilate that he might take away the body of Jesus: and Pilate gave him leave. He came therefore, and took the body of Jesus. And there came also Nicodemus, which at the first came to Jesus by night, and brought a mixture of myrrh and aloes, about a hundred pound weight. Then took they the body of Jesus, and wound it in linen clothes with the spices, as the manner of the Jews is to bury" (John 19:38-40). Do not let your fear of others rob you of the joy of open allegiance. It is sin to be silent when to confess would help another.

To be ashamed of Christ is really a sad experience. It implies carelessness, error, and failure on our part. It dishonors Christ and brings personal defeat.

If Jesus Christ were ashamed of you and me, that we could easily understand; but for men and women to be ashamed of Christ is difficult to comprehend. Joseph Griggs asks,

> Jesus, and shall it ever be
> A mortal man ashamed of Thee?
> Ashamed of Thee, whom angels praise
> Whose glories shine thro' endless days?
>
> Ashamed of Jesus! Sooner far
> Let evening blush to own a star;
> He sheds the beams of light divine
> O'er this benighted soul of mine.
>
> Ashamed of Jesus! That dear friend
> On whom my hopes of heav'n depend!
> No, when I blush, be this my shame,
> That I no more revere His name.
>
> Ashamed of Jesus? Yes, I may,
> When I've no guilt to wash away;
> No tear to wipe, no good to crave,
> No fears to quell, no soul to save.

Ashamed of Christ? We must never be. Repeatedly we are encouraged in Scripture to confess Christ openly and not be ashamed. Jesus said, "Whosoever therefore shall be ashamed of me and of my words in this adulterous and sinful generation; of him also shall the Son of man be ashamed, when he cometh in the glory of his Father with the holy angels" (Mark 8:38). To be reproached for Christ now is to be rewarded later. At times we may be called upon to partake in Christ's sufferings. This really implies that He and we are together. "If any man suffer as a Christian, let him not be ashamed" (I Peter 4:16), writes Peter.

I have found that failure to acknowledge Jesus Christ often results in careless living, but a public commitment puts one on record before God and man. The fact that others know of your decision will really help guard you against temptation.

Yes, your decision is a blessed one. With Philip Doddridge you can sing,

> O happy day that fixed my choice
> On Thee, my Saviour and my God.
> Well may this glowing heart rejoice,
> And tell its raptures all abroad.
>
> Happy day, happy day,
> When Jesus washed my sins away.

Yes, your decision has begun a real, happy, lasting change. You are ready to build a life for God.

WHAT YOU MUST NOW DO

As a newborn baby is cared for in the physical world, you need to be helped spiritually. Let me list four helpful suggestions that I will enlarge upon in later chapters:

1. *Read the Bible systematically*

What food is to the body, the Bible is to your new spiritual life. At a prescribed time, in a quiet place, each day should start with the Bible. This is a must if you are to grow in the things of God. The Gospel of John is a good place for you to begin. Remember, at least a chapter a day! D. L. Moody said, "The Bible will keep you from sin or sin will keep you from the Bible." A chapter a day will help to keep sin away.

2. *Learn to pray*

Prayer is the communion of the believer with God; we speak to God, but He also speaks to us. Prayer is not merely asking favors of God, but rather waiting in quietness before Him. Pray for personal cleansing and victory over evil; pray for yourself and pray for others.

3. *Use every opportunity to confess Christ before the world*

In a winsome way, immediately tell someone of your spiritual decision. Activity always strengthens. When believers share with others, they develop an appetite for Bible study. The result of their speaking to others of their new life will provide daily up-to-date subjects for prayer. When a new Christian begins working, everything comes into proper focus. R. A. Torrey said, "If you make but little of Christ, Christ will make but little of you."

4. *Become part of a local church*

If a mother permits her child to grow up in idleness, the result will be untaught children. Since the Christian's responsibilities toward other believers is evident, waiting only forms bad habits. The Bible says, "Not forsaking the assembling of ourselves together, as the manner of some is" (Hebrews 10:25). Your faithful church attendance will help you in spiritual growth. Join a fellowship that gives full allegiance to Jesus Christ and the Word of God.

If you follow these four Bible steps, Christian growth is guaranteed.

You will be sure to meet temptations, but you need not yield or fall for God has promised, "Greater is he that is in you, than he that is in the world" (I John 4:4). If you do fall, seek immediate forgiveness. "If we confess our sins, he is faithful and just to forgive us our sins, and to cleanse us from all unrighteousness" (I John 1:9). If you fall, do not remain defeated, but get up and go right on. Perhaps right now you are facing the battle with some habit; remember that Christ is ready to help you, and He has all power in heaven and earth.

Another secret of victorious Christian living is to keep your eyes on Christ. The best of men will fail you at times, but never forget—Jesus never fails.

CHAPTER 3

HOW TO BE THE FRIEND OF GOD

FREDERIC HOOD

WE SOMETIMES SPEAK of a time before we were born or thought of. There was of course a time before we were born, but actually there never was a time before we were thought of. God knew each one of us by name from all eternity. He had a separate plan for each of us, but one thing was common to all, for he made us for union with himself. It is God's will that no barrier should exist between any one of his children and himself. We are to love what he loves, hate what he hates, believe what he teaches, choose what he wills. God, who is love, cannot by his very nature compel us to attain to union with him, which is the goal of existence, but he has shown us clearly how we may do so.

The highest activity of free man, which marks one of the chief differences between ourselves and the lower animals, is the capacity for conscious fellowship with God. This discussion aims at giving some idea of how to experience that fellowship; and the author's hope is that the reader will begin, or continue in, a vigorous life of prayer and public worship. To try to apprehend God's plan in any other context would be of little value. The supernatural cannot effectively be experienced from without. And it is surprising how many grown-up people, even though they may sometimes attend church services, have little or no adult devotional lives, and if they say any prayers at all, are still using those which they learned at their mothers' knees.

For convenience, prayer may be classified as vocal and mental, though one shades off into the other, and the distinction is not clear-cut. The former may roughly be said to consist in talking to God, the latter in listening to God, and both are of vital importance. The attitude in which we enter upon prayer is penitence for our share in the present sad state of the world. For this many people today are blaming God, whereas it is in fact the direct result of man's misuse of his free will. And here it should be noted that God in his mercy can bring good out of the very worst of evils; yet nothing is ever obtained by means of sin that could not have been gained better without it.

It is often said that the greatest sinners make the greatest saints, but a little consideration will show that this is not true. St. Paul, St. Augustine, St. Francis, Charles de Foucauld were miracles of supernatural grace; but the greatest saint of all was our Lord himself, and he was without sin. This distinctive Christian outlook is in sharp contrast to current teaching about self-realization. It is commonly said that the experience of sin is needed in order to sympathize with sinners and help them. The truth is that temptation to sin is the experience needed, and that sympathy is likely to be more practically effective when the temptation has been resisted.

The first stage of vocal prayer is Adoration. If we love somebody, our first thought is to please him and delight in his presence, not to ask favors of him. As we approach God, we recognize first his infinite majesty and perfection. Thus, we might begin: "O God the Father, the Almighty, my Creator, I adore thee. O God the Son, Redeemer, Saviour,

Friend, I adore thee. O God the Holy Ghost, living in the Church, illuminating my conscience, I adore thee. O Holy, Blessed and Glorious Trinity, Three Persons and One God, I adore thee."

But in this worship we are not alone. If we only thought of ourselves, we might well be disheartened. The tiny little thread of prayer going up from our bedsides morning and evening would seem so pathetically minute as to be hardly worth continuing. So we will consciously remember the hosts of angels and saints, and the souls of those who have suffered and died; indeed, the whole company of angels and of men within the Church, both on earth and in the worlds beyond.

We shall do well to make friends with some of the saints personally by reading about them and holding converse with them. The great Baptist preacher, Charles Spurgeon, gave good advice when he said, "Speak with the braves, who have won their crowns, heroes who have fought a good fight and now rest from their labours, waving the palm. Let your hearts be often among the perfected, with whom you are to spend eternity" (*The Treasury of the New Testament,* Vol. III, p. 625).

The particular traits of one saint will appeal to each of us more than those of another. We shall think of the thousands who in the last twenty years have gladly accepted torture and death rather than deny their Master. We shall remember friends and relations who have recently died, and that small minority of men and women still living who are called by God to give their whole lives to sacrificial prayer. "I want to join in the worship and adoration which ever goes up before thy eternal throne from the whole Church militant, expectant and triumphant, and from the angelic hosts; from those who have suffered and died for thee in Germany, in Russia, behind the Iron Curtain; from my nearest and dearest lately departed; from the communities devoted to prayer in the world today." We shall thus see ourselves as part of a tremendous whole, limbs in the Body of Christ, and realize that, if we and our friends ceased to pray, something would be lacking in the powerful drive on the side of all that is good as against the forces of evil which are palpably surging round, perhaps as never before.

After Adoration will come Thanksgiving;

> Count your many blessings,
> Name them one by one,
> And it will surprise you
> What the Lord hath done.

Lest we should forget to thank God properly, it is well to have a list of objects for thanksgiving, which will of course need keeping up to date. It will include thanksgiving for our creation, redemption, and protection, for the Church, for health (including eyesight, hearing, etc.), for family, friends, home and food, for all which gives us enjoyment, such as music and works of art, for many answers to prayer, for the sufferings which have taught us sympathy.

It is only at this stage that we can approach Intercession. It may well be that it will rightly occupy most of our time; nevertheless, it is important not to regard it as the sole part of our vocal prayer. Let us consider what exactly we are trying to accomplish by interceding for persons.

Our purpose of course is not to try to drag God's will down to ours, but rather to lift up our wills into union with his. We do not even want the thing we pray for to come to pass, unless it is in full accordance with God's will. The amazing truth is that God allows us to cooperate with him in bringing about what he desires.

Let us suppose that we are praying for our friend, Mrs. X., who has lapsed from the Church and is living in sin. We are deliberately taking time and trouble to lift up our whole personalities into union with our Lord, offering those moments specially for Mrs. X; and thus spiritual energy is released and the trouble we have taken makes it easier for Mrs. X to return. She is not forced to do so, for Love cannot compel. To use a simple analogy; a strong wind may be blowing a man along the street as he walks, but it is open to him to turn round and walk against the wind.

We must not expect always to see the result of our prayers, for God works in a mysterious way. Often in the course of life, results become clear many years later; and when we do see such effects, we must regard these, not as our right, but as a treat by which God in his mercy encourages us.

It is essential to have lists of the persons for which we pray. It is true that we can pray most effectively about matters that interest us; but we must see that our interests are wide enough. It may be hard to pray for foreign missions in the abstract; but if we acquaint ourselves with conditions and needs in some particular part of the mission field, then it becomes a joy to be enabled to share in the work.

Our prayers will be closely linked with what we read in the daily papers. Christians must ever be watchful on the side of God and his righteousness. If we have any enemies or persons toward whom we are tempted to feel bitterness, we shall pray regularly and humbly for these. Even the exercise of our sense of humor will help us to realize that our own shortcomings make us quite unworthy to judge others. The old saying is still true—"You can pray for those you hate, but you cannot hate those for whom you pray."

It may be added that prayer and social service inevitably go hand in hand. If we really mind about slums, unemployment, the gulf between manual workers and the Church, etc., we shall be intelligently praying about them, and this very fact will bring us opportunities to help. There is something sterile and uninspiring about secular philanthropy, without Christian motivation. Inevitably it lacks penetrating perceptiveness, since the insight needed to perform good works effectively comes from patient eagerness to learn God's will in prayer.

Now we turn to mental prayer, or listening to God. Elementary psychology teaches us that the human mind may be compared to an iceberg, which has an immense expanse under the water and little above. Thus, in addition to our conscious thoughts, we have a huge "unconscious" into which impressions are going moment by moment. Between the two is the threshold of consciousness, something like a trapdoor, through which thoughts keep rising up. As things are at present with most of us, when we have nothing special to think of—for instance, in the bus or train on our way to work—the wrong sort of thoughts may present themselves, thoughts of unkindness, jealousy, impurity, etc.

By means of a lifetime of meditation, our object must be so to saturate the whole of our minds in the outlook of our Lord and his saints that to an ever-increasing degree we react to each situation as he would: and the thoughts which emerge into consciousness will be soaked in his love, joy, peace, long-suffering gentleness, etc. Thus, sin is not so much conquered as crowded out. Gradually we become no longer the sort of man or woman who could act as we did before.

The process is not a negative one of laboriously refraining from this or that. Even if we succeeded in doing this, we should only arrive at a pedestrian neutrality. All our prayers should be positive—to attain the virtue which is lacking rather than merely to avoid vice. Our Lord does not call them blessed who just succeed in not breaking the Commandments—those who do not actually murder or steal and commit adultery.

It is the poor in spirit, the gentle, those who are hungry for holiness, the merciful, the pure in heart, the peacemakers, those who courageously face bereavement or unjust persecution, who are commended. He does not say: "Refrain from harming your enemies"; he says, "Love them." This does not of course refer to an emotion which is outside our control, but to an attitude of mind, which in response to grace we can attain. We must be longing not for the condemnation of our enemies but for their conversion and sanctification—and this applies not only to our personal enemies, but to those who have ill-treated our country, our family or our friends. (Charity in the latter cases needs abundant grace.)

Again, our Lord does not say, "Ignore those who hate you; keep carefully out of their way, and put them out of your mind as far as possible." He says: "Do good to them ... pray for them which despitefully use you" (Matthew 5:44 [A.V.]). With Christ there are no half measures. "Ye therefore shall be perfect, as your heavenly Father is perfect" (Matthew 5:48). The result which we wish to attain may be illustrated by a story of the great biblical scholar Johann Bengel. One day he was working far into the night, not knowing that anyone was near; and as he closed his books and prepared to retire, he was heard to say: "Dear Lord Jesus, we're still on the same old terms." That was the thought which rose up instinctively into his conscious mind.

How then are we to set about all this? There is no subject on which generalization is more unwise, for each must find out the method that suits him best. However, all may start by Bible reading in the context of prayer.

Kneel down and put yourself in the presence of God; ask for the guidance and illumination of the Holy Spirit. Banish, so far as may be, the distractions of the world. Then take one of the New Testament books, beginning with a Gospel. Do not feel bound to read any particular number of verses. On one day you may need only one or two, on another a whole chapter. Read on until you can find something to dwell upon and make your own. Try to see within our Lord's mind, and thus to make his point of view your own. (It is often in direct opposition to popular opinion today.) This may lead on to prayer for some virtue, and perhaps to a resolution, which may be carried out in the course of the day.

It is not unusual for even the very young or inexperienced to be able to rest quietly in God's presence, listening to his voice, with only one dominant thought in mind—for instance, God as our Father, our Lord as the Healer of the whole personality, the Holy Spirit, permeating the whole outlook on life. On the other hand, there are many who will always need a book to help them in their meditation. It is a serious mistake to suppose that either of these two classes is more "spiritual" or nearer to God than the other.

An experience for which all must be prepared is dryness at prayer. Indeed, great conscious enjoyment generally comes early in the spiritual pilgrimage, as an encouragement to persevere. But later on for weeks or months we may feel as if God were absent and nothing was happening. If we are to be ready for this, it is vital that we should have a rule of life. Otherwise, when dryness comes, we shall reduce or omit our prayers, with the result that old temptations which we thought were overcome will present themselves in force, and we shall find, with bitter regret, that we have given way.

We are all made up of mind, will and emotions. The first two are largely under our control; but the emotions play all sorts of tricks with us, depending on the state of our health or the weather, or the behavior of our family. Thus, the safeguard is to live by rule. With our minds we decide the subject of our prayer, with our wills we set ourselves to devote a given time to it. Feelings must be left to take care of themselves, provided only that we are sure that no barrier of unforgiven sin is holding up our fellowship with God. The strange truth is that, if our intentions are right, twenty minutes of prayer time that seems quite sterile, may be more effective than the same time spent in happy fellowship with God. It was more costly and thus more sacrificial.

And this leads on to what lies at the back of all that is written above—the truth that *All life should be a prayer.* For the basis of prayer is self-offering. When once we have truly surrendered to Christ, every faculty of our being—body, mind and spirit—is placed at his disposal for twenty-four hours of every day. The test to which each thought and word and deed must be subjected is whether our Lord could experience it with us, suffer it with us, enjoy it with us. This must apply both to work and recreation to every joke we make, to every drink we consume, to every theater we visit. Indeed, the time we spend asleep is equally part of our prayer. Wherever we go in the rough-and-tumble of life, prayer will go up for those among whom we live and move, and this distinctively Christian attitude to life will lead us to exert an influence for good in ways of which we may never know.

CHAPTER 4

HOW TO KNOW GOD

J. I. PACKER

I

WHAT WERE WE made for? To know God. What aim should we set ourselves in life? To know God. What is the "eternal life" that Jesus gives? Knowledge of God. "This is life eternal, that they might know thee, the only true God, and Jesus Christ, whom thou hast sent" (John 17:3). What is the best thing in life, bringing more joy, delight, and contentment, than anything else? Knowledge of God. "Thus saith the LORD, Let not the wise man glory in his wisdom, neither let the mighty man glory in his might, let not the rich man glory in his riches; but let him that glorieth glory in this, that he understandeth and knoweth me" (Jeremiah 9:23 f.). What, of all the states God ever sees man in, gives Him most pleasure? Knowledge of Himself. "I desire ... the knowledge of God more than burnt offerings," says God (Hosea 6:6).

In these few sentences we have said a very great deal. Our point is one to which every Christian heart will warm,

---
From *Knowing God*, copyright 1973, by J. I. Packer, used by permission.

though the person whose religion is merely formal will not be moved by it. (And by this very fact his unregenerate state may be known.) What we have said provides at once a foundation, shape, and goal for our lives, plus a principle of priorities and a scale of values. Once you become aware that the main business that you are here for is to know God, most of life's problems fall into place of their own accord.

The world today is full of sufferers from the wasting disease which Albert Camus focused as Absurdism ("life is a bad joke"), and from the complaint which we may call Marie Antoinette's fever, since she found the phrase that describes it ("nothing tastes"). These disorders blight the whole of life: everything becomes at once a problem and a bore, because nothing seems worthwhile. But Absurdist tapeworms and Antoinette's fever are ills from which, in the nature of the case, Christians are immune, except for occasional spells of derangement when the power of temptation presses their mind out of shape—and these, by God's mercy, do not last. What makes life worthwhile is having a big enough objective, something which catches our imagination and lays hold of our allegiance; and this the Christian has, in a way that no other man has. For what higher, more exalted, and more compelling goal can there be than to know God?

From another standpoint, however, we have not as yet said very much. When we speak of knowing God, we are using a verbal formula, and formulas are like checks; they are no use unless we know how to cash them. What are we talking about when we use the phrase "knowing God"? A special sort of emotion? Shivers down the back? A dreamy, off-the-ground, floating feeling? Tingling thrills and exhilaration, such as drug-takers seek? Or is knowing God a special sort of intellectual experience? Does one hear a voice? see a vision? find strange trains of thought coursing through one's mind? or what? These matters need discussing, especially since, according to Scripture, this is a region in which it is easy to be fooled, and to think you know God when you do not. We pose the question, then: what sort of activity, or event, is it that can properly be described as "knowing God"?

II

It is clear, to start with, that "knowing" God is of necessity a more complex business than "knowing" a fellow-man, just as "knowing" my neighbor is a more complex business than "knowing" a house, or a book, or a language. The more complex the object, the more complex is the knowing of it. Knowledge of something abstract, like a language, is acquired by learning; knowledge of something inanimate, like Ben Nevis or the British Museum, comes by inspection and exploration. These activities, though demanding in terms of concentrated effort, are relatively simple to describe. But when one gets to living things, knowing them becomes a good deal more complicated. One does not know a living thing till one knows, not merely its past history, but how it is likely to react and behave under specific circumstances. A person who says "I know this horse" normally means, not just "I have seen it before" (though, the way we use words, he might only mean that); more probably, however, he means "I know how it behaves, and can tell you how it ought to be handled." Such knowledge only comes through some prior acquaintance with the horse, seeing it in action, and trying to handle it oneself.

In the case of human beings, the position is further complicated by the fact that, unlike horses, people cover up, and do not show everybody all that is in their hearts. A few days are enough to get to know a horse as well as you will ever know it, but you may spend months and years doing things in company with another person and still have to say at the end of that time, "I don't really *know* him at all." We recognize degrees in our knowledge of our fellow-men; we know them, we say, "well," "not very well," "just to shake hands with," "intimately," or perhaps "inside-out," according to how much, or how little, they have opened up to us when we met them.

Thus, the quality and extent of our knowledge of them depends more on them than on us. Our knowing them is more directly the result of their allowing us to know them than of our attempting to get to know them. When we meet, our part is to give them our attention and interest, to show them good-will and to open up in a friendly way from our side. From that point, however, it is they, not we, who decide whether we are going to know them or not.

Imagine, now, that we are going to be introduced to someone whom we feel to be "above" us—whether in rank, or intellectual distinction, or professional skill, or personal sanctity, or in some other respect. The more conscious we are of our own inferiority, the more we shall feel that our part is simply to attend to him respectfully and let him take the initiative in the conversation. (Think of meeting the Queen, or the Duke of Edinburgh.) We would like to get to know this exalted person, but we fully realize that this is a matter for him to decide, not us. If he confines himself to courteous formalities with us, we may be disappointed, but we do not feel able to complain; after all, we had no claim on his friendship. But if instead he starts at once to take us into his confidence, and tells us frankly what is in his mind on matters of common concern, and if he goes on to invite us to join him in particular undertakings he has planned, and asks us to make ourselves permanently available for this kind of collaboration whenever he needs us, then we shall feel enormously privileged, and it will make a world of difference to our general outlook. If life seemed footling and dreary hitherto, it will not seem so any more, now that the great man has enrolled us among his personal assistants. Here is something to write home about and something to live up to!

Now this, so far as it goes, is an illustration of what it means to know God. Well might God say through Jeremiah,

"Let him that glorieth glory in this, that he understandeth and knoweth me"—for knowing God is a relationship calculated to thrill a man's heart. What happens is that the almighty Creator, the Lord of hosts, the great God before whom the nations are as a drop in a bucket, comes to him and begins to talk to him, through the words and truths of Holy Scripture. Perhaps he has been acquainted with the Bible and Christian truth for many years, and it has meant nothing to him; but one day he wakes up to the fact that God is actually speaking to him—him!—through the biblical message. As he listens to what God is saying, he finds himself brought very low; for God talks to him about his sin, and guilt, and weakness, and blindness, and folly, and compels him to judge himself hopeless and helpless, and to cry out for forgiveness.

But this is not all. He comes to realize as he listens that God is actually opening His heart to him, making friends with him, and enlisting him a colleague—in Barth's phrase, a *covenant partner*. It is a staggering thing, but it is true—the relationship in which sinful human beings know God is one in which God, so to speak, takes them on to His staff, to be henceforth His fellow-workers (see I Corinthians 3:9) and personal friends. The action of God in taking Joseph from prison to become Pharaoh's prime minister is a picture of what He does to every Christian: from being Satan's prisoner, he finds himself transferred to a position of trust in the service of God. At once life is transformed. Whether being a servant is matter for shame or for pride depends on whose servant one is. Many have said what pride they felt in rendering personal service to Sir Winston Churchill during the Second World War. How much more should it be a matter of pride and glorying to know and serve the Lord of heaven and earth!

What, then, does the activity of knowing God involve? Holding together the various elements involved in this relationship, as we have sketched it out, we must say that knowing God involves, first, listening to God's word and receiving it as the Holy Spirit interprets it, in application to oneself; second, noting God's nature and character, as His word and works reveal it; third, accepting His invitations, and doing what He commands; fourth, recognizing, and rejoicing in, the love that He has shown in thus approaching one and drawing one into this divine fellowship.

III

The Bible puts flesh on these bare bones of ideas by using pictures and analogies, and telling us that we know God in the manner of a son knowing his father, a wife knowing her husband, a subject knowing his king, and a sheep knowing its shepherd (these are the four main analogies employed). All four analogies point to a relation in which the knower "looks up" to the one known, and the latter takes responsibility for the welfare of the former. This is part of the biblical concept of knowing God, that those who know Him—that is, those by whom He allows Himself to be known—are loved and cared for by Him. We shall say more of this in a moment.

Then the Bible adds the further point that we know God in this way only through knowing Jesus Christ, who is Himself God manifest in the flesh. "... Hast thou not known me...? he that hath seen me hath seen the Father:' "no man cometh to the Father but by me" (John 14:9, 6). It is important, therefore, that we should be clear in our minds as to what "knowing" Jesus Christ means.

For His earthly disciples, knowing Jesus was directly comparable to knowing the great man in our illustration. The disciples were ordinary Galileans, with no special claims on the interest of Jesus. But Jesus, the rabbi who spoke with authority, the prophet who was more than a prophet, the master who evoked in them increasing awe and devotion till they could not but acknowledge Him as their God, found them, called to Himself, took them into His confidence, and enrolled them as His agents to declare to the world the kingdom of God. "He appointed twelve, to be with him, and to be sent out to preach ..." (Mark 3:14, RSV). They recognized the one who had chosen them and called them friends as "the Christ, the Son of the living God" (Matthew 16:16), the man born to be king, the bearer of "the words of eternal life" (John 6:68), and the sense of allegiance and privilege with this knowledge brought transformed their whole lives.

Now, when the New Testament tells us that Jesus Christ is risen, one of the things it means is that the victim of Calvary is now, so to speak, loose and at large, so that any man anywhere can enjoy the same kind of relationship with Him as the disciples had in the days of His flesh. The only differences are that, first, His presence with the Christian is spiritual, not bodily, and so invisible to our physical eyes; second, the Christian, building on the New Testament witness, knows from the start those truths about the deity and atoning sacrifice of Jesus which the original disciples only grasped gradually, over a period of years; and, third, that Jesus' way of speaking to us now is not by uttering fresh words, but rather by applying to our consciences those words of His that are recorded in the gospels, together with the rest of the biblical testimony to Himself. But knowing Jesus Christ still remains as definite a relation of personal discipleship as it was for the twelve when He was on earth. The Jesus who walks through the gospel story walks with Christians now, and knowing Him involves going with Him, now as then.

"My sheep hear my voice," says Jesus, "and I know them, and they follow me" (John 10:27). His "voice" is His claim, His promise, and His call. "I am the bread of life ... the door of the sheep ... the good shepherd ... the resurrection" (John 6:35; 10:7, 14; 11:25). "He who does not honour the Son does not honour the Father who sent him. Truly, truly, I say to you, he who hears my word and believes him who sent me, has eternal life" (John 5:23 f., RSV). "Come unto me, all ye that labour, and are heavy laden, and I will give you rest. Take my yoke upon you, and learn of me ... and ye shall find rest ..." (Matthew 11:28 f.). Jesus' voice is "heard" when Jesus' claim is acknowledged, His promise trusted, and His call answered. From then on, Jesus is known as shepherd, and those who trust Him He knows as His own sheep. "... I know them, and they follow me; and I give unto them eternal life; and they shall never perish, neither shall any man pluck them out of my hand" (John 10:27 f.). To know Jesus is to be saved by Jesus, here and hereafter, from sin, and guilt, and death.

IV

Standing back, now, to survey what we have said that it means to "know thee, the only true God, and Jesus Christ, whom thou hast sent," we may underline the following points.

First, knowing God is a matter of *personal dealing,* as is all direct acquaintance with personal beings. Knowing God is more than knowing about Him; it is a matter of dealing with Him as He opens up to you, and being dealt with by Him as He takes knowledge of you. Knowing about Him is a necessary precondition of trusting in Him ("how could they have faith in one they had never heard of?" [Romans 10:14, NEB]), but the width of our knowledge about Him is no gauge of the depth of our knowledge of Him. John Owen and John Calvin knew more theology than John Bunyan or Billy Bray, but who would deny that the latter pair knew their God every bit as well as the former? (All four, of course, were beavers for the Bible, which counts for far more anyway than a formal theological training.) If the decisive factor was notional correctness, then obviously the most learned biblical scholars would know God better than anyone else. But it is not; you can have all the right notions in your head without ever tasting in your heart the realities to which they refer; and a simple Bible-reader and sermon-hearer who is full of the Holy Ghost will develop a far deeper acquaintance with his God and Savior than more learned men who are content with being theologically correct. The reason is that the former will *deal with God* regarding the practical application of truth to his life, whereas the latter will not.

Second, knowing God is a matter of *personal involvement*, in mind, will, and feeling. It would not, indeed, be a fully personal relationship otherwise. To get to know another person, you have to commit yourself to his company and interests, and be ready to identify yourself with his concerns. Without this, your relationship with him can only be superficial and flavorless. "O taste and see that the Lord is good," says the psalmist (Psalm 34:8). To "taste" is, as we say, to "try" a mouthful of something, with a view to appreciating its flavor. A dish may look good, and be well recommended by the cook, but we do not know its real quality till we have tasted it. Similarly, we do not know another person's real quality till we have "tasted" the experience of friendship with him. Friends are, so to speak, communicating flavors to each other all the time, by sharing their attitudes both towards each other (think of people in love) and towards everything else that is of common concern. As they thus open their hearts to each other by what they say and do, each "tastes" the quality of the other, for sorrow or for joy. They have identified themselves with, and so are personally and emotionally involved in, each other's concerns. They feel for each other, as well as thinking of each other. This is an essential aspect of the knowledge which friends have of each other; and the same applies to the Christian's knowledge of God, which, as we have seen, is itself a relationship between friends.

The emotional side of knowing God is often played down these days, for fear of encouraging a maudlin self-absorption. It is true that there is nothing more irreligious than self-absorbed religion, and that it is constantly needful to stress that God does not exist for our "comfort," or "happiness," or "satisfaction," or to provide us with "religious experiences," as if these were the most interesting and important things in life. It is also necessary to stress that anyone who, on the basis of "religious experiences," "saith, I know him, and keepeth not his commandments, is a liar, and the truth is not in him" (I John 2:4; cf. verses 9, 11, 3:6, 11, 4:20). But, for all this, we must not lose sight of the fact that knowing God is an emotional relationship, as well as an intellectual and volitional one, and could not indeed be a deep relation between persons were it not so. The believer is, and must be, emotionally involved in the victories and vicissitudes of God's cause in the world, just as Sir Winston's personal staff were emotionally involved in the ups and downs of the war. The believer rejoices when his God is honored and vindicated, and feels the acutest distress when he sees God flouted. Barnabas, when he came to Antioch, "and had seen the grace of God, was glad" (Acts 11:23); by contrast, the psalmist wrote: "rivers of waters run down my eyes, because they keep not thy law" (Psalm 119:136). Equally, the Christian feels shame and grief when convicted of having failed his Lord (see, for instance, Psalm 51, and Luke 22:61 f.), and from time to time knows transports of delight as God brings home to him in one way or another the glory of the everlasting love with which he has been loved ("transported with a joy too great for words" [I Peter 1:8, NEB.]). This is the emotional and experiential side of friendship with God. Ignorance of it argues that, however true a man's thoughts of God may be, he does not yet know the God of whom he is thinking.

Then, third, knowing God is a matter of *grace*. It is a relationship in which the initiative throughout is with God—as it must be, since God is so completely above us and we have so completely forfeited all claim on His favor by our sins. *We* do not make friends with *God; God* makes friends with *us,* bringing us to know Him by making His love known to us. Paul expresses this thought of the priority of grace in our knowledge of God when he writes to the Galatians, "now that you have come to know God, *or rather to be known by God* ..." (Galatians 4:9). What comes to the surface in this qualifying clause is the apostle's sense that grace came first, and remains fundamental, in his readers' salvation. Their knowing God was the consequence of God's taking knowledge of them. They know Him by faith because He first singled them out by grace.

"Know," when used of God in this way, is a sovereign-grace word, pointing to God's initiative in loving, choosing, redeeming, calling, and preserving. That God is fully aware of us, "knowing us through and through" as we say, is certainly part of what is meant, as appears from the contrast between our imperfect knowledge of God and His perfect knowledge of us in I Corinthians 13:12. But it is not the main meaning. The main meaning comes out in passages like the following:

"And the LORD said unto Moses ... thou hast found grace in my sight, and *I know thee by name*" (Exodus 33:17). "Before I formed thee (Jeremiah) in the belly *I knew thee;* and before thou camest forth out of the womb I sanctified thee" (Jeremiah 1:5). "I am the good shepherd, *and know my sheep,* and am known of mine ... and I lay down my life for the sheep ... My sheep hear my voice, *and I know them* ... and they shall never perish" (John 10:14 f., 27 f.). Here God's knowledge of those who are His is associated with His whole purpose of saving mercy. It is a knowledge that implies personal affection, redeeming action, covenant faithfulness, and providential watchfulness, towards those whom God knows. It implies, in other words, salvation, now and for ever, as we hinted before.

V

What matters supremely, therefore, is not, in the last analysis, the fact that I know God, but the larger fact which underlies it—the fact that *He knows me*. I am graven on the palms of His hands. I am never out of His mind. All my knowledge of Him depends on His sustained initiative in knowing me. I know Him, because He first knew me, and continues to know me. He knows me as a friend, one who loves me; and there is no moment when His eye is off me, or His attention distracted from me, and no moment, therefore, when His care falters.

This is momentous knowledge. There is unspeakable comfort—the sort of comfort that energizes, be it said, not enervates—in knowing that God is constantly taking knowledge of me in love, and watching over me for my good. There is tremendous relief in knowing that His love to me is utterly realistic, based at every point on prior knowledge of the worst about me, so that no discovery now can disillusion Him about me, in the way I am so often disillusioned about myself, and quench His determination to bless me. There is, certainly, great cause for humility in the thought that He sees all the twisted things about me that my fellow-men do not see (and am I glad!), and that He sees more corruption in me than that which I see in myself (which, in all conscience, is enough). There is, however, equally great incentive to worship and love God in the thought that, for some unfathomable reason, He wants me as His friend, and desires to be my friend, and has given His Son to die for me in order to realize this purpose. We cannot work these thoughts out here, but merely to mention them is enough to show how much it means to know, not merely that we know God, but that He knows us.

CHAPTER 5

HOW TO READ THE BIBLE

CLAUDE H. THOMPSON

I LIKE THE SPIRIT of the man who, I have heard, begins the day with the prayer, "Good morning, Lord. What are you up to today? I'd like to be a part of it."

As enthusiastic as he may be, however, unless he reads the Bible regularly and carefully, he will miss out on most of what God is really doing.

Why read the Bible and not some other good book?

The answer is that the Bible is a record of God's search for man, and of man's oft-repeated blundering response. It is the account of how God brought a special people into being, and how the Christian community got started. And in it all there is the majestic and moving story of the one Man who stands tallest among the sons of men, Jesus Christ of Nazareth.

In a peculiar way the believer finds in the Bible a living witness to the life of God—set forth in Jesus and available to

---

Reprinted by permission from CHRISTIAN LIFE Magazine. Copyright September 1970 Christian Life Inc., Gunderson Dr. & Schmale Rd., Wheaton, IL 60187.

all who dare to follow Him. Whenever a person comes to the Bible, with his life open to the influence of the Holy Spirit, the written Word becomes the vehicle to provide the "implanted word" (James 1:21)—to convey God's message to him. Jesus Himself says, "You search the Scriptures, because you think that in them you have eternal life; and it is they that bear witness to me" (John 5:39).

But my task is not to argue for the superiority of the Christian's Bible. It is simply to answer the question, "How can I read the Bible for help?" I give my suggestions in outline form with little comment, trusting that they will be of some aid to the honest seeker after biblical truth.

1. The Bible should be read in the Spirit and practice of prayer.

This is basic. Prayer and Bible reading go hand in hand. John Wesley urged that, prior to reading the Scriptures, this prayer should be prayed:

> Blessed Lord, who hast caused all holy Scriptures to be written for our learning; Grant that we may in such wise hear them, read, mark, learn, and inwardly digest them, that by patience and comfort of thy holy Word, we may embrace, and ever hold fast, the blessed hope of everlasting life, which thou hast given us in our Savior Jesus Christ. Amen.
> (Collect for the Second Sunday in Advent, *Book of Common Prayer.*)

Prayer prepares the person, by mellowing his life, to respond to the written Word of God. It sensitizes his inner being to hear the whispers of the Spirit Who aided in the preparation of the Bible in the first place. Nothing is more important. Nothing can supplant this necessary discipline for Bible reading.

In our living room is a picture produced by a Korean artist, who used the total words of the New Testament, about 185,000 of them. After printing the complete text, he darkened certain words to outline the figure and features of Jesus so that our Lord stands out within the printed words of the New Testament message. So, to use the expression of E. Stanley Jones, the words of the Bible do not merely become printer's ink; they are "the Word become flesh." Jones often comes to his reading of the New Testament with the Greek words as they spoke to Philip: "We would see Jesus." Thus the prayer of the believer is that the Word of Jesus Himself may come to him out of the printed text of the Bible. This is what prayer ought to do as we come to the Holy Scriptures.

2. *Various translations and paraphrases should be used.*

For a modern-language translation of the New Testament, I like J. B. Phillips. His *Letters to Young Churches* have made the epistles come to life for many people. And, of course, Phillips' complete translation of the New Testament along with portions of the Old Testament have brought the message of the Bible into our modern words.

Also, in *Good News for Modern Man,* the American Bible Society has put the New Testament into the language of our time—and the pen sketches contribute greatly to the interpretation of the message.

Among the paraphrases, Ken Taylor's *Living Bible* has been particularly helpful to young people.

The Cotton Patch Version of Paul's Epistles, paraphrased by the late Clarence Jordan, may be a bit shocking for traditional readers, especially those with a racist outlook. But Jordan seems to catch something of the rough and vigorous mood of Paul. For example hear these:

> Now get this straight: Even if we or an angel fresh out of heaven preaches to you any other message than the one we preached to you—to hell with him (Galatians 1:8). Now if somebody thinks he is a big shot when he is nothing but a nubbin, he is kidding himself ... Don't let anybody pull the wool over your eyes—you can't turn up your nose at God! (Galatians 6:3, 7).

If someone objects to this stinging language, he should go to the Greek text for a careful exegesis. Remember also that the New Testament was written in the colloquial language of the street of the times—not in an antiseptic study or ivory tower.

We need the whole counsel of God. Therefore, we must be sure to include the Old Testament in our Bible reading.

And now this fall comes the complete New American Standard Bible, produced by the new publisher, Creation House, Inc. This is the only full text of the Bible translated into contemporary language by a team of American scholars since the American Revised Version of 1901. It is bound to be read with great interest.

Certainly at no point in history have there ever been so many helpful translations of the Bible, and there is no excuse today for a superficial understanding of the Holy Scriptures.

3. *The use of a lectionary is important.*

This is a list of suggested readings for each day of the year—often for both morning and evening. Such a list often follows the Church Year or calendar. I use the one from the *Book of Common Prayer* of the Anglican Communion, but many other churches have prepared such guides. The one issued by the American Bible Society is especially good. The lectionary helps in a systematic reading of the most meaningful parts of the Bible and aids in avoiding those parts which have little relevance for our time. But perhaps one of the most important reasons is that it encourages a regular reading of the Scriptures rather than a hit-and-miss occasional method.

4. *The Bible should be read aloud.*

We ought to hear the Bible with our ears as well as read it with our eyes. The late Charles Laughton found in the Bible a powerful dramatic medium for expressing human emotions—under God. The moving poetry of the Psalms, the drama of the people of God, the personal witness of the letters, the dialogues with Jesus, the appeals of the sermons, even the judgment of the laws—all become more meaningful when *heard* as well as *seen*.

Of course, not the least important reason to hear the Bible

is that in this manner it is more easily memorized. Then when we are without a copy of the printed Word, we may still "read" it for ourselves.

In recent years the Bible has been recorded and is available for play-back purposes. The Bible Voice organization has all the quotable portions of both the Old Testament and the New Testament on records and tapes as well as cassettes.

5. *We need the aid of commentaries.*

It is not completely true that the Bible is its own interpreter. The findings of the scholars are needed to give background material, to help interpret difficult passages, and to relate the ancient message to modern life.

One of the most helpful for New Testament study is *The Daily Study Bible,* a series prepared by William Barclay of Scotland. *The Layman's Bible Commentary,* published by John Knox Press, represents not only reverent scholarship but a warm evangelical spirit. Some persons may want more involved works such as *The Interpreter's Bible* or *Harper's New Testament Commentaries.* And surely a good atlas is needed.

6. *In small reading groups each person can share insights within the fellowship.*

Some books, such as *Job* and *Ruth*—or the *Psalms,* for that matter—may easily be read in dialogue. The records of the *Acts of the Apostles* are especially suited for group reading. Some of the letters could be read as they were originally intended to be used—directed to the community of faith. This easily precipitates a discussion as to the application for our times. And an in-depth study of some involved section, such as *Revelation,* often proves valuable when done within a study group.

7. *There should be an unhurried reading of the Bible.*

A "quiet time," particularly in the morning, is most important. A relaxed, receptive mood is needed. Time and again a passage which, at first reading, seems obscure, suddenly will grow with new meaning. There is really no way to explain this except through the Holy Spirit.

8. It should be read with pen and pad in hand.

This unhurried reading of the Bible will enable us to write down insights which just "seem to come." These are recorded for meditation and study. In this manner, the Bible reader prepares his own "commentary." This is not a device simply for preachers hunting sermon leads. It is for everyone. Some of the most meaningful insights into the application of the Bible have come to me in my devotional reading—and writing.

9. The Bible is a transcript of life in every generation.

It was written out of life itself to reflect the living conditions of the time—but it fits any situation of any time. In this respect it is the most contemporary of all books.

The Bible is a revolutionary book. It will make communism look tame—if we only will dare to subject the social evils of our time to the demands of the Gospel! The Bible is a transcript of life in every generation—including ours.

10. It should be read with the inner life completely open to the Holy Spirit.

Completely open—for God to do as He desires with us! It was Luther who urged that the Holy Spirit is the greatest teacher of the Holy Scriptures. An academic approach to the Bible is important. I have spent my life in this discipline. But there is a depth of understanding beyond the most thorough technical study possible. And sometimes a purely scholarly analysis has interfered with a vital understanding of the Bible.

Thus in reading the Bible, we should be prepared for a revolution! For if we expose our lives to the hearing of the living Word of God and obey it, we little know how the Holy Spirit may direct us.

CHAPTER 6

HOW TO TAKE HOLD OF THE BIBLE

DON FIELDS

HAVE YOU EVER ASKED yourself, "Why doesn't the Bible find its way into my life more frequently?" I have. We hear other Christians speaking about what the Scriptures mean to them, but perhaps it just isn't our experience. With a little bit of work, we can correct this.

How can we apply Scripture to our lives? Learning involves three steps. First we *observe* and try to see what the facts are; next we *interpret,* trying to make some kind of order out of the facts; finally we *apply* by finding an appropriate course of action.

Why has God given us His Word? Because it is His basic tool to conform us to the image of Jesus Christ. All Bible study should lead us to the question, "What does God want me to *do* about the truth He has shown me?" I don't believe we really learn anything until we are implicated by some course of action that involves us in the truth. In that involvement (prompted by the Holy Spirit) God teaches us and changes us to become like His Son.

Copyright 1970, by HIS Magazine, used by permission.

A PLAN

Let me share a plan that helps me to begin this process. Each week I pray that God will take one passage out of Scripture and make it real to my own life. During the week as I am reading according to some program, I analyze each day's passage by putting it into my own words. My goal is to get it into terms common today. In the course of the week one passage will particularly impress me, and on that passage only, I use an A-B-C approach. I *A*nalyze the portion as I described it above. Then I choose the *B*est verse, and usually memorize it. After this I usually make a *C*ontract. I find that Scripture breaks down into three main areas: commands to obey, promises to claim, principles to practice. My contract is related to one of these. I get a little squeemish at this point, because I know it is getting personal and I might have to do something.

The problem becomes one of leaving the general and coming to the specific. We often shoot at nothing—and hit it everytime—in our Bible study application. I usually ask myself a couple of questions. Where did I miss this in my life? Where can I practice or put this into effect in my life? Nail your course of action down. Make it so specific that you can't get out from under it. If God spoke to you about loving the people on your dorm floor, don't pray, "Lord, help me to love everyone on my dorm floor." Say, "Lord, remind me to pick up my clothes because my roommate is a meticulous person and my sloppiness bugs him." Or, "Lord, remind me to turn down the stereo when my roommate is studying because he can't concentrate," or, "Lord, remind me to turn the lights off at a reasonable hour when my roommate is trying to sleep." When you get this specific you are involved. We should not say, "I should," "I ought," "I must," etc., but "by your grace I will ..."

Find someone who can share applications with you so that you can be more objective and also get help from a friend with your problem. Also, write your applications down so that you will have them for future reference. At the rate of making one contract a week, I find that I can't work on more than three contracts at a time or it becomes frustrating. So I periodically cross off some contracts as I add others. God can bring one I've crossed off to my attention again when that is necessary. Often I find that God will repeat the same application for several weeks with slight variations.

SOME EXAMPLES

Here is a personal illustration to show how I do this in my life. A lady in California is a close friend of mine. After seminary we corresponded fairly regularly. Once she wrote me about an elderly woman in Terre Haute who was having a hard time making ends meet. She needed some help because she had no contact with relatives or churches. I wasn't scheduled to visit Terre Haute for quite a while, so I wrote a letter to the president of the local I-V chapter asking him to look into the matter. Immediately I forgot it.

A month went by and no letter came from my California friend. This second month a letter came. It started out like this: "My Dear Precious Brother ..." This woman is a real exhorter, and I knew something was coming ... "I want to stir you up about a common sin of young preachers and Christian workers today ... that is the sin of *neglect!*" (She took one whole line across the page to write this last word.) My first reaction was, "My dear woman, if you only knew how much work I have to leave undone because I simply don't have the time to do it ..." Since God had used this woman to speak to me many times before, however, something said I had better calm down before doing or saying anything.

The next morning I came across Proverbs 25:12, "Like a gold ring or an ornament of gold is a wise reprover to a listening ear." Ouch! I was writing an application that morning and immediately started to generalize. I told God that I was thankful that He had shown me this truth. I said I would try to do better in the future. God reminded me that I already knew I was to do better. The question was, What was I going to *do* about it? I could find no peace until I made a long distance telephone call and found out what had happened to the woman. In this case she had been taken care of. I also had to sit down and write a letter to my friend, saying, "You are right, I am guilty of the sin of neglect." I memorized that verse in the hope that it would deter me from practicing the sin of neglect the next time.

I don't know what your application will be. You may need to make an apology. You may need to write a letter. Maybe you should memorize the verse or passage and review it every day for two weeks. Possibly you could pray about the area every day for two weeks. God will tell you what He wants you to do, but don't just stop with the truth itself. Go on to that course of action which will drive the truth into your life. In that way the Word of God will start to mold your life to the likeness of Jesus Christ.

CHAPTER 7

HOW TO EXPERIENCE THE TRANSFORMING POWER OF THE SPIRIT

J. OSWALD SANDERS

> "But we all, with open face beholding as in a glass the glory of the Lord, are changed into the same image from glory to glory, even as by the Spirit of the Lord"
> (II CORINTHIANS 3:18)

READING: II CORINTHIANS 3:1-18

"HOW MAY WE ACQUIRE likeness to Christ?" This verse provides a satisfying answer to this wistful question of many hearts. There is not only one answer to that question, for there are many varieties of Christian experience, and the fullness of blessing is not experienced by all in the same manner or through the same aspect of truth. But this paragraph sets out in unmistakable terms one of the great secrets of conformity to the image of Christ.

The context of this alluring possibility draws a striking contrast between the old covenant of law and the new covenant of grace—the passing glory of the one, the

---

From *Spiritual Maturity*, copyright 1962, by Moody Bible Institute, used by permission.

surpassing splendor of the other—between Moses and face veiled, and the believer with veil removed. The requirement of the old covenant was that man, by his own unaided effort, should live up to the exacting standard of God's holiness in the decalogue, a requirement which led only to deep despair. The supreme revelation of the new covenant was that transformation of character into the likeness of Christ comes not by painful striving, but by beholding and believing and the operation of the Holy Spirit in the heart of the believer. The old covenant which came by Moses was a ministration of death and condemnation, but the new covenant which was ushered in by the death of Christ was a ministration of righteousness and life (vv. 7, 8). The aspiration of Moses under the old covenant was expressed in his request, "I beseech thee, show me thy glory." The realization of this aspiration in the new covenant is seen in the text, "we all, with unveiled face, beholding ... the glory of the Lord are changed into the same image."

AN OBJECTIVE VERSION

"We all with open [unveiled] face beholding as in a glass the glory of the Lord." Transformation of character begins not with subjective introspection, but with an objective vision of the glory of the Lord and the Lord of glory. It is "Christ Jesus, who of God is made unto us sanctification [holiness]" (I Corinthians 1:30). And where may this captivating vision be seen? Not in illuminated heavens but in the written Word—the mirror which reveals His perfect manhood, His flawless character, His unique Person and His mediatorial work. Concerning the Word of God, Jesus said, "Search the scriptures ... they are they which testify of me" (John 5:39). Paul asserts that "the light of the knowledge of the glory of God" may be seen "in the face of Jesus Christ" (II Corinthians 4:6). But where can that face be authentically seen? Not on a painter's canvas, for the most beautiful painting is only the projection of the artist's conception of

Christ. It can be seen only in the records of His inspired biographers who under the guidance of the Holy Spirit have given us with meticulous accuracy a full-length portrait of Him.

The Jews saw the Face, but they missed the glory because a veil lay over their minds, a veil of prejudice and hatred and unbelief far more impenetrable than the veil which concealed Moses' radiant face (v. 7). But, says Paul, through Christ this veil is taken away (v. 14). And now "we all"—not a select group of especially holy people—"with unveiled face" may gaze at His glory. The glory here referred to is, of course, the moral glory of Christ, His excellences of character and conduct, which shine out everywhere in the Scriptures.

A SUBJECTIVE TRANSFORMATION

"Are being changed into the same image." This objective vision has a subjective purpose, that we might be changed into His likeness. God is not satisfied with us as we are. Nor are we satisfied with ourselves as we are if we really know ourselves. The Son of Man was to the Father such an object of delight, He so perfectly fulfilled all His purposes and conformed to His standard, that He plans for all His children to be "changed" or, as the word is, "transfigured" into His likeness. When our Lord was transfigured before His disciples, for a moment He drew aside the veil of flesh which concealed His innate and essential glory and allowed the three on the mount to briefly glimpse it. "We beheld His glory, the glory as of the only begotten of the Father," said John several decades later. "We were eyewitnesses of His majesty," said Peter, another of the favored three on the mount of transfiguration. We have no such inherent and essential glory. The Divine purpose for us is not mere external imitation but internal transformation. And the transformation will not be transient and evanescent. We shall not lose the glory as did Moses. "The children of Israel could not steadfastly behold the face of Moses for the glory of his countenance; which glory was to be done away" (v. 7). Ours is to be glory retained and transmitted. "For if that which is done away was glorious, much more *that which remaineth* is glorious" (v. 11).

And the method of transformation? "Beholding." Not a despairing struggle against that which captivates, but a steady, concentrated gazing on Christ and a confident relying on the Holy Spirit to effect the change.

The word used here for "beholding" may with equal propriety be rendered either "beholding" or "reflecting." As we behold His glory, we are changed into His likeness. As we are changed, we reflect as in a mirror the image into which we are transformed. Reflecting is the inevitable result of beholding.

It is a law of life that we become like those we constantly gaze at. The eye exercises a great influence on life and character. The education of a child is conducted largely through the eye. He is molded by the manners and habits of those he constantly sees. This is the explanation of the powerful influence of the movies on young people. They become like that on which they gaze. Look on the streets of a large city and you will see counterparts of famous actresses. Their fans copy them in dress, in speech, in behavior. We become like those we admire. Alexander the Great studied Homer's *Iliad* and as a result he went out to conquer the world. William Cowper, the celebrated poet, when a young and sensitive boy, read a treatise in favor of suicide. Who can doubt that when, later in life, he attempted to destroy himself, it was the influence of the book which had gripped him in earlier days. In the spiritual realm, how many famous preachers have numerous smaller editions of themselves among their admirers!

On one occasion the writer was holidaying at an isolated spot. When the Lord's Day came, the only church service of any kind was conducted by a Salvation Army soldier, an illiterate farmer. His text was the one at the head of this chapter. He was not eloquent. He did not evidence deep learning. Some of his exegesis was questionable. But his reiteration of his text etched four words indelibly on the mind—"*beholding, we are changed.*" His radiant face and obvious joy in the Lord were exemplification of the truth of his claim. A glance of faith may save, but it is the gaze of faith which sanctifies, said Robert Murray McCheyne. A hurried glance at Christ snatched after lying abed too late will never effect a radical transformation of character.

Dr. A. B. Simpson sees us here as the photography of God, the Holy Spirit developing and perfecting Him in the midst of our lives. If the image is to be perfect, the sitter must be in focus. The veil must be removed. The sitter must remain quite still with steadfast gaze since it is a time exposure. After the image has been transferred to the sensitive film in the moment of exposure, there follows the process by which the acids etch away all that conceals the likeness of the subject. This is the ministry of the Holy Spirit who, as we yield to His influence, removes all that is unlike Christ and imparts to us His own perfections.

But we are also to *reflect* the glory of the Lord as Moses did after his forty days' sojourn in the mount in the presence of the glory of God. When we behold the glory of Christ in the mirror of Scripture, His glory shines upon us and into us, and then is reflected by us. With Moses it was a transient and fading reflection of the glory, but it need not be so with us. It should be our constant aim to ensure that we are an accurate reflection of Christ to the world of men around us. It is very possible for His image in us to be distorted and blurred in the course of transmission, as our own image has been in a fun-fair mirror. Since unbelieving men can know Christ only by what they see of Him in us, how important that we do not misrepresent Him, that we do not display our own carnal attitudes instead of His moral beauty and glory. What they see of Christ reflected in us should turn their antagonism and indifference into wistfulness and faith.

A PROGRESSIVE EXPERIENCE

"*We are being changed* into His likeness from one degree of glory to another." Translators render this sentence differently, but in them all there is the idea of progression. "Through successive stages of glory," "in ever increasing splendor," "from a mere reflected to an inherent glory," "from one degree of radiant holiness unto another." One thing is clear. It is not the purpose of God that our Christian experience should be static. There lie ahead of us endless possibilities of growth into the likeness of Christ. These words clearly show that Christlikeness in all its fullness is not the result merely of some moment of high and holy exaltation, but that it is a progressive experience. The inward change produced in us by the Holy Spirit is to be daily transforming us more nearly to the image of our Lord. We are transfigured by the renewing of our minds.

THE TRANSFORMING AGENT

"Even as by the Lord the Spirit." "The Lord the Spirit," as it is in the original, is an unusual phrase and poses a theological problem. William Barclay comments: "Paul seems to identify the Risen Lord and the Holy Spirit. We must remember that Paul was not writing theology; he was setting down experience. And it is the experience of the Christian life that the work of the Spirit and the work of the Risen Lord are one and the same. The strength, the light, the guidance we receive come alike from the Spirit and from the Risen Lord. It does not matter how we express it so long as we experience it."

We need to see in this transformation our responsibility and the Holy Spirit's ministry. The change into the likeness of Christ is not automatic. It involves moral endeavor and activity. We are not only to "let go and let God," we are also to "put off" and "put on" certain things, and this involves definite activity of the renewed will. It is not the inevitable result of passive daydreaming about Christ. Our part is to "behold the glory of the Lord" in active, expectant faith. The Spirit then exercises His prerogative of revealing the glory of Christ and reproducing that likeness in ever increasing splendor. We behold Him, but we trust and expect the Holy Spirit to change us into Christ's likeness. The transforming work is entirely His as He ministers and imparts to us all the values and virtues of the Person and work of Christ. We behold in silent adoring contemplation; He works into the fabric of our lives what we see in Jesus.

In achieving this, the Spirit exercises both a negative and a positive ministry. First, *He reveals to us the things in our life and character which are unlike Christ,* and therefore must go. Everything alien to the perfection of Christ must be "put off." This revealing ministry is not pleasant, indeed it can be devastating, for despite our protestations of unworthiness we are all greatly biased in our own favor. We do not enjoy others evaluating us as we profess to evaluate ourselves. But if we sincerely desire to be transformed, we will be willing to part with everything that mars Christ's image in us. God cannot "put off" these manifestations of unlikeness to Christ. It is something which we alone can do, and must do. Paul indicates elsewhere things which must be put off if we are to be assimilated into Christ. "Anger, wrath, malice, blasphemy, filthy communication out of your mouth. Lie not one to another" (Colossians 3:8-9).

But the Spirit not only reveals what must be discarded. He enables us to do it. "If ye *through the Spirit* do mortify the deeds of the body, ye shall live," were Paul's bracing words (Romans 8:13). We are not left to our own unaided efforts as were those who lived under the old covenant. We have a mighty Paraclete whose supreme delight it is to aid us to the limit when our hearts are set on becoming like Christ in character and conduct.

Then *the Holy Spirit reveals the graces and blessings which should and could be ours,* and enables us to appropriate them. One of the tragedies of many Christian lives is the poverty of their experience when contrasted with the vastness of their unclaimed privileges. "Blessed be the God and Father of our Lord Jesus Christ," wrote Paul, "who *hath* blessed us with *all* spiritual blessings ... in Christ." "*All things* are yours." "According as his divine power *hath given* unto us *all things* that pertain unto life and godliness." There is no grace which we behold in the character of our Lord which may not be ours in increasing measure as we look to the Spirit to produce it in us.

"Beholding ... we are changed."

PART II
LOVING OTHERS

INTRODUCTION

In a very real sense we cannot love others without first loving God. Until we are brought into an awareness of divine love we can only express a rudimentary form of love, which is likely to have more in common with shallow affection or gratification than sacrificial giving. As Christians we have responded to God's supreme offer of love. But our membership in His household is no guarantee that we will fulfill the second part of the great commandment, "You shall love your neighbor as yourself" (Matthew 22:39).

Many factors work against our being able to love others: personality conflicts, the depersonalization of modern society, demands others make on time we want (or need) to ourselves, the ill-will some people bear towards us, and a host of others. Even in the family, the basic social institution ordained by God, love of others is a struggle. Edith Schaeffer believes the key to love between family members is balance. In "How to Live in a Family and Like It" she compares the family to a seesaw; it works on the principle of give and take. It becomes unbalanced and hence inoperative if one member selfishly looks after his own needs without regard for the rest of the family.

A real index of our love of others is our willingness to share God's gifts to us. In "How to Be a Wise Steward of God's Gifts" Charles Ryrie explains that what we do with our money matters. We should give to others sacrificially because God has given to us sacrificially. Moreover, we are to think of the blessings we receive from God—time and talents as well as money—in terms of *stewardship*, not ownership. We possess nothing; all is God's; we are servants, not masters. It is only through faithful stewardship that we can hope to be inheritors of the Kingdom. Similarly, in "How to Overcome the Time Trap" Bob Sheffield proves that even the busiest people can make their time count for eternity.

If we have been able to approach even a shadow of God's love for us in our love for one another, what do we do when someone close is taken from us? This is the problem Elisabeth Elliot deals with in "How to Face the Death of a Loved One." Having lost one husband to martyrdom at the hands of South American Indians and another to the "excruciating disintegration" of cancer, Elisabeth Elliot has indeed borne her share of grief. Yet it is the knowledge that Another bore all our sufferings on the Cross that helps her triumph over sorrow.

In turning to issues about Christian life-style, L. Nelson Bell explains why Christians ought to show forth in their lives evidences of their regeneration in Jesus Christ. In "How to Act Like Christians" he notes among these evidences sympathy, compassion, courtesy, and patience. If we don't have values like these to show for our salvation, the world will certainly question its worth.

When Christians forget that what unites them is greater than what separates them, it often leads to trouble. What a sorry spectacle when Christians quarrel with each other! Yet Church history is full of disagreements between Christians, a disturbing number of them leading to violence. Robert Webber in "How to Get Along with Other Christians" puts forth the view that the key to Christian cooperation is mutual affirmation of *the truth* that binds all Christians together into one body, even though emphasized differently within various traditions. Christians must become practiced in "speaking the truth in love" (Ephesians 4:15).

Howard A. Snyder is also concerned with how Christians

INTRODUCTION

relate to each other. In "How to Deepen Church Life Through Small Groups" he advances the hypothesis that the move toward ever-larger congregations results in the loss of the kind of true, deep, rich Christian fellowship experienced by the early Church. The small group provides an ideal setting for the reconciling and renewing work of the Holy Spirit.

Otis Young tried a radical experiment in his congregation. A pastor of a typical suburban church, he asked his members to come to a meeting that would be aimed at "nothing less than a complete reorientation to all life." He invited them to come and share their deepest concerns, to ask their most troubling questions, to make themselves vulnerable. The response he received and the results achieved through God's power had lasting effects in his church.

The following chapters offer abundant evidence that loving others is a goal that can be achieved by most Christians in most situations—if we open ourselves to the ministering of the Holy Spirit, and if our will is conformed to God's.

J. P. D.

CHAPTER 8

HOW TO LIVE IN A FAMILY AND LIKE IT

EDITH SCHAEFFER

> Seesaw, Margery Daw,
> Jacky shall have a new m-aaa-ster,
> And he shall have but a penny a day,
> Because he can't work any f-aaa-ster!

W<small>HISH</small> – B<small>UMP</small> – W<small>HISH</small> – B<small>UMP</small> – *whish – bump – creak – creak – whish – bump!*

"How well they balance each other, Margotty and Elizabee. Look at them go!"—"Now it's our turn. Hurry up, Kirsty, you get there and let me hang on to it here—ooops—Help!" Becky finally gets herself astride, too, and off they go, hair flopping up and down, the singsong chant coming out in breathless little jerks, *"Seesaw, Margery Daw...."*—"Push harder. I almost don't go up again. Push with your feet when you hit; I can't get down!"—"*And he shall have but a....*"—"Now put Giandy on with Jessica—ooops—It won't work otherwise. Look, just one big thud, and Jessica is up in the air and can't come down. You

---

From *What Is a Family?*, copyright 1976, by Edith Schaeffer, used by permission.

have to balance the weight. It's just no good without a balance of weight!"—"*Seesaw, Margery Daw, Jacky shall have a new m-aaa-ster."*—"You need a little help there to keep the balance right. Here. I'll help, because I can give just that extra little push at the right moment. There you go!" *Whish – bump – whish – bump – whish – bump!* "A little help was all you needed to get your feet off the ground again, and to bring the other one down again. It's the *balance* that counts."

It's the balance that counts all through life. It's the balance that matters in the Christian life. It's the balance that matters in human relationships. It's the balance that matters in *family life*. There is a delicate balance, like the equal weight of two people seesawing, or like someone walking a tightrope. Too much on one side, too much on the other, and there comes the thud of one person on the seesaw or the fall of the person on the rope—the continuity of what was going on comes to a sudden stop. Balance is the very important ingredient in every area of life. We see unbalanced people ruining their own lives by being exaggerated in one area or another. We feel upset when we notice a person we love going off on a tangent of one kind or another. We criticize Christian positions or political views which we feel are lopsided and all out of balance. Yet, so often we are in danger of being blind to the lack of balance in the places where it makes the greatest of difference to ourselves as personalities—to the person closest to us, to our families, to our children, if we have them, to our parents, to our grandparents, to our friends. We are not only in danger of hurting or disturbing other human beings by our lack of balance, but we can, as children of the Living God, bring dishonor to the Lord in our lack of balance.

We are meant to be representing the Lord as His children. Look at Malachi 1:6: "A son honoureth his father, and a servant his master: if then I be a father, where is mine honour? and if I be a master, where is my fear? saith the Lord of hosts unto you, O priests, that despise my name...."

When we accept Christ as our Saviour, we become sons of God as well as servants and priests, and in each of these capacities we are meant to bring honor to God by the way we represent Him to others. If we make no attempt to be balanced in our Christian lives and in our family lives, we are very poor representatives and are in danger of bringing dishonor to the Lord. Second Corinthians 5:20 says we are also "ambassadors for Christ," another vivid description of our need to represent Him well before a watching world. Proverbs 13:17 declares to us, "A wicked messenger falleth into mischief: but a faithful ambassador is health." It isn't simply what we *say* with a good balance which matters. Our lives, our actions, our relationships, our family life, and the wider influence which our family can have as an example to others, *must* have some balance which does not leave one thing "up in the air" and the other "flat on the ground" like a seesaw with two unmatched people as far as weight goes!

Are any of us perfectly balanced? Do I think *I* am? No, of course not. We are imperfect, sinful, full of mistakes, with much to learn until Jesus comes to take us to be with Him, in changed bodies with the sins and imbalances gone! But in this, as in other imperfections, we are called upon to strive for growth and change, and we are meant to help each other "get off the ground" or "come down out of the air." Does nagging and pointing out faults help? A thousand times *no*, but through prayer and gently adding weight on one side or another, we can sometimes help each other—without being obnoxious. As mothers and fathers of children, as grandparents or aunts or uncles, we have responsibility in the area of the need for balance to pray with an awareness and to try to help with as much sensitivity as possible. Parents need to realize that their children, even very young children, can sometimes come out with very wise words in pointing out an inconsistency or an imbalance. There is a humbleness needed in all directions as we live, "each esteeming the other better than themselves" (*see* Philippians

2:3). The *other* can be child, parent, father, mother, grandmother, grandfather—in two directions! The call of the Lord is for us to be sensitive to our difficulty in keeping a balance, and to look to Him for help. Surely the need for balance is to be taken literally in His promise: "If any of you lack wisdom, let him ask of God, that giveth to all men liberally, and upbraideth not; and it shall be given him" (James 1:5). We are also warned to remember literally, "For the wisdom of this world is foolishness with God ..." (I Corinthians 3:19). There *will* be ideas concerning family life and family togetherness which will be infiltrating us, as Christian parents, which come from *this* world and are complete foolishness with God.

As a Christian who believes the Bible to be really true, I do believe we are in a battle and that we have an enemy—Satan. If it is true that Satan hates God and wants to destroy everything that God has made, then *of course* Satan would want to destroy the family. The family is basic. God made man and woman. The first balance that was given was before sin entered into the relationship, a *perfect* balance of two being one, spiritually, intellectually, and physically. All the imbalances have come as a result of sin upsetting the perfect balance, whether in ecological areas of nature or in human relationships. Anytime there is any "danger" (in Satan's way of looking at it) of anything having a possibility of being back *in balance,* Satan, of course, would strike out to destroy that balance. All the disrupting influences and twisted, warped ideas of what a family ought to be, are not simply "chance results" of the century we are in because of the process of evolution! It is quite the opposite—there is a plan behind the devastating falling apart of the family. There is a person behind the plan who wants the family units to fall apart.

One of the most clever blows to the existence of the family is the attempt to destroy the antithesis (or the reality of opposites existing) in the very basic polarity that was made

How To Live In A Family

by God—the existence of male and female as different, but fulfilling each other and having the possibility of being one, with the added possibility of bringing forth new human beings who are a blend of the two. The blow against enhancing and enjoying the *differences* between men and women, making it a "dirty word" to say that there *are* differences, and striving for "unisex" in every aspect of personality, is a blow against one of the most beautiful and delicate of all balances. What is being done to men and women is to push one "up in the air" with the other one "down on the ground," with Satan's foot planted on the end of the seesaw, so to speak! Satan is laughing his head off at the struggle to get free from his foot, as he watches Christians as well as non-Christians fall into the confusion of the declaration he sets forth in a flood of books, papers, magazines, movies, lectures—all saying that there is no male-female difference, and that there *must* not be. Poor, trembling people on top of the seesaw, hair blowing in the breeze, fearful as the breeze whips into a wind, not knowing how to get down! People are "up in the air" because of the lack of balance in anything they have been taught, and struggling not to recognize what they feel inside of themselves—struggling against the feminineness of being a woman, struggling against the masculineness of being a man, trying to feel neuter. The unfair weight is being put on by a clever intelligence who can slip out of sight!

As Christian couples, as Christian parents, as Christian grandparents, as aunts and uncles who are Christian, we have a responsibility to help in keeping very clear the beauty of the balance of differences. Marvelous to have a father who is a rock, a strong tower, a defense against attack, a counselor, a shelter against enemies. Wonderful to have a mother who is able to concentrate on teaching, being sensitive to the child's need, compassionate and warm and cuddly and providing the atmosphere of home in the very way of serving food, or making clothing, of doing some of those things pointed out in Proverbs 31 as making a woman the kind of person she should be. Wonderful to have communication with both parents contributing, in agreement, yet with slightly different angles of understanding. What a need there is for teaching little boys that it is great to be a boy "because you will be a father and love and care for children of your own." What a need for teaching little girls that it is wonderful to be a mother "because you can bring forth a baby that will grow in your own body, and feed it at your breast."—"No, the father can't feed the baby at his breast, and no, he can't bring it forth out of his body after nine months of growing there, because God made man and woman to have different parts in the matter of being parents."—"Yes, the baby is half of each person because the seed is planted by the father and is as much a part of him as of the mother. While the father is doing other things to get the home ready for the baby and preparing wonderful things for the baby to enjoy, and ways the baby can learn, the mother is free to have the baby right inside her, and have that be one of the very important things she can do."—"Just think, Jonathan, every person who has ever lived has had a mother and a father involved in making him. And the only person who has ever been different is Jesus—who *always* lived and who did something amazing in coming from heaven to be born of Mary, but without a human father." There is a balance—men *and* women. There is another balance—each individual with something of each of the parents.

God shows us that the Heavenly Family, the people who will be in heaven, has two relationships that are meant to be understood easily because of our knowing something true in this life. We will all be one Family, with God the Father as *our* Father, and we will all be the bride of Christ, a composite bride made up of the whole body of believers. Christ is masculine in what is ahead of us, and of our positions *now* as Christians—and we are all feminine, all believers.

What then is to be the *balance* in the truth of the man being the head of the home? The pastor (or undershepherd) of a church should represent Christ who is the Head or the Shepherd. The representation is of the masculine: Bridegroom, Shepherd. The husband is to be the head of the home. How does the head behave? Insofar as possible in ways that represent Christ who is the Head of the church. "Husbands, love your wives, even as Christ also loved the church, and gave himself for it" (Ephesians 5:25). What did Christ do as He gave the commission to His bride, the church, when He left to prepare the place for us to go? His commission was: "Go ye into all the world, and preach the gospel to all creatures [or to all nations]" (*see* Mark 16:15). Christ as the Head gave the most important work that could possibly be done through the centuries to His bride—not to angels, not to Himself in a series of trumpet announcements, but to the church. What loving confidence and trust Christ puts in us—"the bride!" Husbands are to treat their wives as Christ treats the church, which means a very special balance of giving important commissions and handing responsible decisions to the wife. Wives are to reverence their husbands and be subject to them, but as the church is to Christ. It is to be real and to be practical, but with an amazing reality of communication and trust. There is another balance that has to be combined at the same time—the balance of our being "brothers and sisters in Christ"—all one in the Family of God. Husbands and wives are to pray together and with their children in this relationship of being brothers and sisters in the Lord's Family. To do other than this is to usurp the place of God as our Heavenly Father. Of course a child must grow to a place of being old enough to understand the Lord's guidance, but certainly that is not to be when life is almost over!

In some universities no man can become "Professor" until the head of the department dies or retires. Then one man can move up to the top place. In some banks there is a line of hopeful "future presidents" waiting for someone to die, so that they can move up. This is not the understanding of what it means to be able to behave as a child of God, with freedom to ask His will to be unfolded directly to you. You do not need to die before your child can look directly to the Lord. The husband does not have to die before his wife can ask the Lord to show the family His plan, and to ask that the husband will recognize it, too. Our mouths are not covered with adhesive tape in our communication and pleading with the Living God. He is our Father. Christ is our Bridegroom, and we *do* have an Advocate, *now*. The beauty of a family—hand in hand and praying together, having communication together, with this factor recognized insofar as it is possible in the midst of human weaknesses—is marvelous.

An earthly father and mother should *tremble* to take the place of the Heavenly Father or the Shepherd Jesus or the Holy Spirit in telling their children what to do or whom to marry, what university they must attend, what profession they should follow, or whether or not they should go into Christian work. Obedience to God is not a matter of waiting until one's parents die. My father is ninety-nine, and had I needed to let only him make my decisions, I would not yet be ready to ask God what His plan was for me or my family. The balance is delicate; there is a very fine line of difference in weight when suddenly the seesaw flops down and one realizes that the time has come for the "brother or sister in Christ" (one of our own children) to stand directly before the Lord.

Which of us has the wisdom to plan another's life? I feel strongly hit by God's powerful words to Job and to any who would usurp God's direction of His own children, "Then the Lord answered Job out of the whirlwind, and said, Who is this that darkeneth counsel by words without knowledge?" (Job 38:1, 2). What a picture of each of us when we try to plan another person's life, as we "darken counsel by words without knowledge." It couples itself in my mind with, "... If therefore the light that is in thee be darkness, how great is that darkness!" (Matthew 6:23). Yes, I know that false religions are the "dark light," but men's certainty at times of what someone *else* should do can also be a very dark light handed to another person for the path ahead. Who but God can know the future and choose His place for any of His children? Who but God can weave the threads of our lives where they belong in His tapestry?

> Where wast thou when I laid the foundations of the earth? declare, if thou hast understanding.... Where is the way where light dwelleth? and as for darkness, where is the place thereof ...? Knowest thou it, because thou wast then born? or because the number of thy days is great? (Job 38:4, 19, 21).

Do any of us pretend that we have understanding that can compare to God's? How *dare* we try to be the Holy Spirit or the Father in heaven, in our telling others that we know what they should do! People are so prone to tell their own children (but some deign to tell others' children, too) when they should *go* or *stay* or *do this* or *do that*. Is there then no place for talking things over together, for praying together, for helping each other in the area of decisions? Yes, of course, and this is one of the next balances to discuss.

One of the places in danger of becoming pushed out of balance in this century of family relationships is the area of *dependence* versus *independence*. Some accept without questioning the drive for independence as being necessary and good. Some parents feel their greatest responsibility is to teach their children independence. They push a child off their laps with a feeling of great virtue, "I'm teaching him to be independent." Later these same parents don't bother to answer letters when their children are away: "They have to learn how to get along without us." They push a child away when he comes in fear or with questions: "Run along now, you have to find things out for yourself." They pointedly go away when a child is weeping, and never try to find out what is wrong: "Put out your light and go to sleep," and then feel proud of saying to some other adult within hearing, "I'm making her self-sufficient." All signs of dependence are squashed by some parents as quickly as possible: "Give the baby a cup as soon as possible, so he or she won't depend on the bottle for comfort." Breast-feeding is put aside by some as an unnecessary beginning of dependence upon the mother. "Get in a baby-sitter who is new every time, and walk out without any explanation!" is the method some use in order to wean the child away from depending on the mother or father. Any tiny leaf growing on the little plant of communication is pulled off as a sign of dependence.

Yet later in life these *same* parents will sit alone in old-folks' homes or in nursing homes or in lonely apartment houses, while their "independent" children let the parents also be "independent." Is this what a family is all about? Isn't there something upside down—in the call for men to be independent of their wives, wives to be independent of their husbands, children to be independent of their parents, and vice versa? People—afraid of dependence on people. Where is the balance?

"Hearken unto me, O house of Jacob, and all the remnant of the house of Israel, which are borne by me from the belly, which are carried from the womb ... and even to hoar hairs will I carry you: I have made, and I will bear; even I will carry, and will deliver you" (Isaiah 46:3, 4). God is speaking to Israel, but also to all who are in His family. His own children. God is stating very strongly that from before birth and to very old age we can be dependent upon Him, and are meant to be dependent upon Him. "Then shalt thou call, and the Lord shall answer; thou shalt cry, and he shall say, Here I am ..." (Isaiah 58:9). Not only are we to be dependent, but we can cry out to Him, and He will listen and *answer*—not just yell, "Go to sleep."—"For this God is our God for ever and ever: he will be our guide even unto death" (Psalm

48:14). And in Romans 4:20, 21 we find that Abraham didn't stagger at the enormity of God's promises because he believed that what God promised, He "was able also to perform." Abraham lived depending on God.

Family life through the years should be a beautiful and blended balance of dependence upon each other. The security that comes in the midst of dependence gives birth to the right kind of independence. A child is meant to learn by the dependability of the mother's and father's interest and concern that God is a Father who can be depended upon. When God promises guidance, His strength is our weakness, availability, comfort in our sorrows, love, understanding, compassion—these things should have been found on a human level as real elements in the relationship with parents. A very false picture is being given of God when parents push children away in a frenzy of teaching independence as the greatest thing to be learned. What's wrong with dependence of husband upon wife, wife upon husband, child upon parent, parent upon child, grandparent upon grandchildren, grandchildren upon grandparents? All the hue and cry about a "separate identity" and "I don't know who I am apart from this circle of people," is adding weight to the other side of the seesaw and brings the danger of "throwing you up in the air," out of balance.

"I can always depend on my mother understanding what I want to do."—"Really? You mean your mother will let you make that tent with her blankets?"—"Yeah, she understands what we're playing. She just—well, she just understands. Wait and see. I bet she'll give us something to eat, too—to eat in the tent."

"I can depend on my dad to see how much I need to be with him next week. He'll take me along. I just gotta talk because I'm all mixed-up about something!"—"You mean your dad would believe you need to go that bad? He knows it when you need him? Boy!"—"Yeah, there are times when he needs *me*, too; he says so. We like to be together."

"I've got a terrific idea. I want to talk it over with you, Mother. It's an idea for making these...."—"Hey, Mom, come and see what I just made!"

Do you drop things and go? Is it important to you? Are you available? Are you glad for the dependence on you and not afraid of it? Are you dependent, too? Is there someone you want to have see the picture you painted, the book you wrote, the cake you baked, the garden you planted, the doghouse you built—and get his or her opinion on it first? Do you have someone you depend on for giving constructive criticism, but never "missing the point" altogether?

Who am I? I am a human being made in the image of God—who needs horizontal relationships and horizontal dependence on other human beings, just as I need dependence upon God. I don't need to spend my whole life in isolation wildly looking for an identity apart from everyone else. What's wrong with being interrelated with the people my career puts me with—my career as an ecologist, an artist who is involved in making a mobile (living, changing, never the same for two days in a row), my career as a collector for the museum of memories! What's wrong with my identity blending in a mélange, a beautiful mix as mother, wife, sister, friend, counselor, nurse, artist, cook, interior decorator, and so on! Why can't I be interwoven with *people,* since I am a *person?* The impersonality of a separate identity can be terrifying in the way it is carried out in some people's drive to be independent.

The thought that warm, loving human dependence on other members of a family through the years is a "crutch," is a parallel to thinking that if human beings need God, that too, is a "crutch." Both thoughts are born out of an impersonal base, a universe of chance which has no personal Creator in whose image people have been made. In such a universe each person is an independent collection of molecules.

Another balance that is important to consider—as your children plan, fight, or squabble, and you sigh, wish for ten years to pass, look at the clock and wish it was night, or lie in bed wishing the day to pass because you have the flu—is the balance between the danger of wasting the "now," or of considering that everything is going to be static, with no future! It is so easy for people to let their children grow up without being taught to think of the preciousness of "today" and "this hour." I used to stop my children and say over and over again (so many times that each one remembers it as one of the outstanding sentences heard in childhood), "Don't waste this hour. Don't waste today. Stop fighting for a minute and just think! You are getting older every day, and you won't be four, with an eight-year-old sister and a tiny baby sister for very long. Think hard—what can you do now in this combination that you can't do in ten years, in five years, even next year? Then *do* it!"

"You won't be fifteen with an eleven-year-old sister and a seven-year-old sister and a new baby brother for very long. Think! What does this summer have for you and what does today have that you can do, that won't be possible five years from now, two years from now, next week?"

"Figure out what you might wish you had taken time to do. Enjoy each other now. Someday all that you can do today or this week will be only a memory. Let it be a memory of what you *did* do—not of time wasted in fighting."

"What if we have to move; what would you want to do first? What do you enjoy about this garden, this house, these books, that if it all were taken away, you'd wish you were here to do for just one hour? Pretend that this is your last day together in this house, and think what you'd want to play together or look at together. Don't waste the 'now.' "

"I wish I were rid of diapers. Ugh! When this stage is over I'll be glad!"—"I wish I were rid of the preschool years. I'll be glad for a free number of hours!"—"I wish I were finished with teenagers. I can't wait till I can start a new life!"

Diapers also mean a baby stage that is all-too-soon finished, of dear "first" things—first responses, first words, creeping, bits of personality showing through and making you eager for the next stage of finding out who this new person is! Each stages goes so quickly, and life is soon gone. The danger of wasting the "now," because of sighing, quarreling, or being irritated into disregarding any of the positive things which will soon be gone, is a danger of being down at the bottom of the seesaw in an important balance.

What is the opposite danger in this particular blend of balances? *Whish – bump – whish – bump*. What should be balancing the sensitivity to the "now?" It is the recognition that life is not static, that there are things to be discovered in each other, in our selves, in hidden talents and new interests, in freedom to do things which cannot be done now. The attention to be paid to the "now" should be balanced by the inner realization that there is a future with new things ahead. What is the "now" simply won't last, and the changes ahead should be like contemplating wrapped gifts with hidden contents!

"Optimist," I can hear someone say. Perhaps the changes are illness, accident, war, or death. Yes, realistically, yes! This is a fallen world, and the future is not promised as a rosy one, but as Christians we look forward to a final future which is to be fantastic—and until that moment we look forward to God's unfolding of His plan, day by day, in *whatever* set of difficult circumstances. The balance to be considered is the importance of the "now" versus the fact that this present situation isn't static. Within a family, help is needed by each in remembering this. And the toddler can get the idea and help Grandmother, as well as the other way around.

"Who do you suppose Grandfather will want to see first when he gets to heaven?"—"Maybe Grandmother or maybe his parents, because they died so very long ago, or maybe his little boy who died when he was a baby. I guess he might want to see that baby first."—"I don't think so," said Samantha, with her brown eyes round and solemn. "I think he'll want to see God first, 'cause he's never seen Him before." This is the balanced expectation of a four-year-old's view of Grandfather's future!

Another balance needed in the family circle is a planned withdrawing back into another century, balanced by understanding today's world and the philosophy which permeates it. There should be times of reading aloud together books which take the whole family into another period of history, so that a particular historic time becomes as vivid as the newspapers and the news magazines make today's moments, day by day. It is important to discuss and to consciously bring out things of past periods, not as "golden periods" when there was perfection, but to show what is being lost, and what totally wrong standards are being accepted today—accepted simply because they are taken for granted. This doesn't need to be a lecture, but a balancing which is planned by choosing books and times to read them together. Past, present, future—with a blend of understanding based on biblical standards. Balance to help judgment.

The balance of understanding that we need each other across the age gaps is something to teach by seeing that there are some periods of "together times" for the three or four generations of your own family, or by bringing in other people of different ages for your children to be with. It is important to experience being needed by children on the part of old people, and being needed by old people on the part of children, as well as important to find out that there is much to learn in cross-conversation.

The togetherness of generations must also be balanced, however, by a very hard-and-fast rule of never telling young families how they are doing it wrong, if the "mix" is to continue. "Don't give that child that dish of food. Half of it goes on the floor!" is simply no sentence for a grandmother or mother-in-law to say. It's the mother's business if half the food is lost, and a sister or a friend or anyone else has no business in making such a suggestion. The beauty of generations enjoying each other can be destroyed by this kind of interference. Does it work both ways? Well, someone has to be willing to bite his or her tongue and not snap back, and it *ought* to be the older and more experienced person who realizes that the relationship is more precious than showing how "inconsistent" the younger ones are being in their criticism!

Balance must be kept between "putting the Lord first" as someone else might recognize it, and "putting the Lord first" by sufficiently putting the family first. For a family to break up—because the husband or wife or both are "putting the Lord first" in some kind of Christian work—to the extent that the children are never "first" and the marriage relationship is never "first"—is *not* "putting the Lord first." He has given us the responsibility of caring for continuity in oneness and family life.

God speaks to us clearly of fulfilling the sexual needs regularly in marriage, "... that Satan tempt you not for your incontinency" (*see* I Corinthians 7:1-5). And Deuteronomy 6:7—"And thou shalt teach them diligently unto thy children, and shalt talk of them when thou walkest by the way, and when thou liest down, and when thou risest up"—means that children are to be *with* parents. These two passages specifically put the togetherness of husband and wife and the togetherness of the family in a place of *balanced* importance. People seem to ignore the need of thinking of this balance and act as if all Christian men are eunuchs, Christian wives without sexual need, and that the children can be put aside in the press of "first things first." The balance of what is "first" is pretty tragically upset in the overall picture of a particular family's history, and there may be the kind of crash which takes place when someone jumps off a seesaw while someone else is up in the air!

Children need to grow up having the example of responsibility which is exhibited by the father and mother not deviating from a task that has to be done. However, that must be balanced by putting absolutely everything aside for a moment when the whole family or one individual has some special need. Is this "putting everything aside" to be saved for severe illnesses, accidents, death, and funerals? No, but it must be something important and take place infrequently enough to be really impressive as to the importance of what was put in place of the normal work. When Franky was about fifteen, he and his father were having a stormy discussion during which Fran suddenly decided that he had not spent enough time with Franky. Since his trip to Florence with the three girls had been the summer of Franky's birth, the time to go with Franky was not "when it might be convenient," but right away. "But, Dad, would you cancel everything you were going to do in your work for a whole ten days just to go with *me*?" It was such an unusual putting aside of normal responsibilities that nothing could have been as great a demonstration of really caring. That father-son time of seeing the museums of Florence and Venice together—discussing and talking alone over a tremendous variety of things without interruption—was priceless in their relationship. Nothing but time, taken when it is needed, can fulfill a need that takes *time*. Giving a piece of time is much more of a gift in a human relationship within a family than giving a sum of money.

The "putting everything aside" can be a very drastic necessity when the marriage is threatened, and there is a break on the horizon! Years ago Fran visited a couple and found that the husband was packing to leave in the morning. His intention was to go off with a girl from his place of work with whom he was infatuated. Fran stayed all night talking. Not that he was very welcome! But he was able to point out some of the complications of the breakdown of continuity in life: being separated from the children, trying to keep two homes going, grasping for "happiness," when very obviously the problems in the marriage hadn't been discussed, nor had any solution been looked for. By morning the answer was, "Okay, I'll do what you've suggested and give it a try." Because the basic trouble was withdrawal and coldness in the physical part of the marriage, and a seeming lack of understanding in that area on the wife's part, Fran's advice was, "Let Edith talk to your wife, and then you go and *give up your job*, go away for a three-week honeymoon. Go somewhere you've never been before and really do the things you'd enjoy together—without your children for this time. Give your wife money to buy a 'wedding trousseau' and whatever Edith tells her to get."

The next day I spent several hours with the wife while I did my washing and ironing, talking about the biblical view of sex in marriage, not an ascetic view, but one of fulfilling each other's needs. Hers had been a stiff Mid-Victorian up-bringing. I advised her to get an exotic black nightgown and others, some sexy underwear, some very different types of daytime clothes, have her hair done in a completely new style, buy a new kind of perfume, and go off on *his* planned second honeymoon determined to really forgive her husband. She was to start with the realization that she had also been at fault and was prepared to make a completely new beginning. It was a drastic putting aside of job, time, and bank account—with no security for the future together. But—there took place the most amazing discovery of each other as almost unknown people. "Wow, I never knew my wife before! I don't know what was the matter with me." For both it was a willingness to do a seemingly foolish thing for a very wise reason. The balance of putting the most important thing first, and of being willing to lose everything materially, in order to find each other, was a balance that anyone looking on without understanding might call an "irresponsible act"—or an "unbalanced decision."

These people are grandparents today, with a beautiful

family. The material insecurity plunged into at that time has been balanced by the wonderful security of a continuity of family life into the third generation. It is worth it to fight for a variety of *blended balances,* so that the continuity of family life doesn't suddenly come to an abrupt stop! If a job is taking you into dangerous waters as far as your family life goes, be willing to have a lesser job, rather than push on heedless of the greater price to be paid—coming to a split which incidentally breaks the whole picture which families are to *be* of the continuity of the Heavenly Family.

The holiness of God and the love of God are perfectly balanced.

> ... God sitteth upon the throne of his holiness (Psalms 47:8).

> We have thought of thy loving-kindness, O God, in the midst of thy temple (Psalms 48:9).

> God hath spoken in his holiness ... (Psalms 60:6).

> Hereby perceive we the love of God, because he laid down his life for us ... (I John 3:16).

In the death of Christ as He took our place, the love of God and the holiness of God met for us. This God is our Father: "At the same time, saith the Lord, will I be the God of all the families of Israel, and they shall be my people" (Jeremiah 31:1). He is our Father and the God of our families as we become His children.

> For this cause I bow my knees unto the Father of our Lord Jesus Christ, Of whom the whole family in heaven and earth is named (Ephesians 3:14, 15).

> Fear thou not; for I am with thee: be not dismayed; for I am thy God: I will strengthen thee; yea, I will help thee; yea, I will uphold thee with the right hand of my righteousness (Isaiah 41:10).

> For this God is our God for ever and ever: he will be our guide even unto death (Psalms 48:14).

We have a perfectly balanced Father who is also our God,

and who has promised us the help that is needed. He knows we are weak, and He promises us His strength. What a balance—His strength in our weakness! He knows there will be times when we will be afraid for ourselves and for our children—and He promises to be with us so that we don't need to be dismayed. He knows we are in danger of falling flat—and promises to "uphold" us! He hasn't promised us an easy time without suffering, but has promised comfort to balance the suffering. He hasn't said our lives will be smooth, but has promised to give victory in the terrific varieties of battles ahead of us. As we contemplate what a family can be in the twentieth century, there is no need to turn away in discouragement: *For this God is our God for ever and ever: he will be our guide* [yours and mine] *even unto death.*

The original Artist of the mobile—the perfectly balanced art form in constant movement, the living, changing family—is God who made people in His image and placed them together in families held together by invisible threads! Satan, the vandal, has been working at destroying this artwork ever since! The need to "work at it," as with any other art form, is augmented by the need to give protection to the family, to place "guards" to keep the destructive attacks away, and to keep sensitive watch for any approaching army with swords raised to "cut the threads."

A family—for better or for worse, for richer or for poorer, in sickness and in health! Dirty diapers, chicken pox, measles, mumps, broken dishes, scratched furniture, balls thrown through the windows, fights, croup in the night, arguments, misunderstandings, inconsistencies, lack of logic, unreasonableness, anger, fever, flu, depressions, carelessness, toothpaste tops left off, dishes in the sink, windows open too far, windows closed tight, too many covers, too few covers, always late, always too early, frustration, economies, extravagance, discouragement, fatigue, exhaustion, noise, disappointment, weeping, fears, sorrows, darkness, fog, chaos, clamorings—families!

A family—for better or for worse, for richer or for poorer, in sickness and in health! Softness, hugs, children on your lap, someone to come home to, someone to bring news to, a telephone that might ring, a letter in the post, someone at the airport or station, excitement in meeting, coming home from the hospital with a new person to add, someone to understand intellectually, spiritually, emotionally, happy shrieks of greeting in which you are involved, beloved old people, welcomed babies, increasing togetherness, blending ideas of interior decoration, blending musical tastes, growing interests, fun, satisfaction, enjoyment, clean washing, ironed clothing, tulips up, flowers arranged, rugs vacuumed, beauty, dogs, cats, candlelight, firelight, sunlight, moonlight, fields with someone to walk with, woods with someone to picnic, sharing food, imaginative cooking, exchanging ideas, stimulating each other—families!

A family is a mobile strung together with invisible threads—delicate, easily broken at first, growing stronger through the years, in danger of being worn thin at times, but strengthened again with special care. A family—blended, balanced, growing, changing, never static, moving with a breath of wind—babies, children, young people, mothers, fathers, grandparents, aunts, uncles—held in a balanced framework by the invisible threads of love, memories, trust, loyalty, compassion, kindness, in honor preferring each other, depending on each other, looking to each other for help, giving each other help, picking each other up, suffering long with each other's faults, understanding each other more and more, hoping all things, enduring all things, never failing! Continuity! Thin, invisible threads turning into thin, invisible metal which holds great weights but gives freedom of movement—a family! Knowing always that if a thread wears thin and sags, there is help to be had from the Expert—the Father—"Of whom the whole family in heaven and earth is named."

CHAPTER 9

HOW TO BE A WISE STEWARD OF GOD'S GIFTS

CHARLES C. RYRIE

ONE OF THE MOST IMPORTANT evidences of true spirituality is seldom discussed in books or sermons on the subject. We are prone to paint the image of spirituality in colors of deep Bible knowledge, lengthy times of prayer, or prominence in the Lord's work, which is not only deceiving but must be very discouraging to the average believer who can never envision these features as being a part of his life. He concludes, therefore, that these major manifestations of spirituality will never be seen in his life.

To be sure, a vital spiritual life is related to fellowship with the Lord in His Word and prayer and to service for the Lord in His work. But our love for God may be proved by something that is a major part of everyone's life, and that is our use of money. How we use our money demonstrates the reality of our love for God. In some ways it proves our love more conclusively than depth or knowledge, length of prayers or prominence of service. These things can be

---

From *Balancing the Christian Life*, Copyright 1969, by Moody Bible Institute, used by permission.

feigned, but the use of our possessions shows us up for what we actually are.

GIVING

The Apostle John links money and the love of God: "But whoso hath this world's good, and seeth his brother have need, and shutteth up his ... [heart] from him, how dwelleth the love of God in him?" (I John 3:17). This verse is preceded by one which says we ought to lay down our lives for the brethren in order to give the ultimate proof of love. But, of course, most Christians will never have the opportunity to do this even if they would seize the opportunity if it came. How, then, can the believer in ordinary circumstances show that he loves his brother and thus God? The answer is simple: By giving money and goods to his brother. If he fails to do this, then he shows not only that he does not love his brother but also that he does not love God. There is scarcely anyone who cannot give; therefore, all can show by this means the measure of their love for God. Giving of money and things is a manifestation and responsibility of a truly spiritual life.

How, then, do we properly discharge this responsibility?

Without apology the New Testament places a great deal of emphasis on the subject of giving. There are commands, practical suggestions, warnings, examples and exhortations concerning this important ministry. Everywhere in the Bible miserliness, greed and avarice are denounced; and generosity, hospitality and charity are extolled. Money is not a carnal or worldly subject to be avoided or spoken of only after "more important" matters have been considered. The same word that is used for our fellowship with the Lord is also used in relation to the fellowship of collecting money (II Corinthians 8:4). This clearly underlines the spiritual character of giving. Furthermore, giving is a spiritual gift (Romans 12:8) which is available to all believers to have and to use. And it is a gift which all Christians can exercise regardless of the individual's financial status.

There is always a tendency when we read the Bible passages that speak of money or rich people to apply them to someone else. We invariably look at the person in the next higher income bracket and transfer the teaching of such passages to him. We too easily forget that there is someone in the next lower income range who is looking at us and applying the teaching to us! Each of us is a rich person to someone else; therefore, these teachings apply to all of us.

What should be one's guide in grace giving? Undoubtedly the New Testament passage which sets forth most concisely the basic principles of giving is I Corinthians 16:2: "Upon the first day of the week let every one of you lay by him in store, as God hath prospered him, that there be no gatherings when I come." In this single verse are laid down four principles of giving.

1. Giving is incumbent on each person—"let every one of you."

Grace does not make giving optional; it is the privilege and responsibility of every Christian, and it is the concrete manifestation of his love for God. Giving is a personal matter in which every believer sustains a direct and individual responsibility to the Lord as if he were the only Christian in the world. What you give is your personal business just as long as you are giving and doing it in conference with Him before whom all things are naked and open.

2. Giving is to be proportionate—"as God hath prospered him."

No hard and fast rule concerning the amount is to be found among New Testament principles of giving. This is in sharp contrast to the regulations of the Old Testament which required that a tenth of all be given to the Levites (Leviticus 27:30-33), who in turn tithed what they received and gave it to the priests. In addition, the Jews understood that a second tithe (a tenth of the remaining nine-tenths) was to be set apart and consumed in a sacred meal in Jerusalem (Deuteronomy 12:5-6, 11, 18; those living too far from

Jerusalem could bring money). Further, every third year another tithe was taken for the Levites, strangers, fatherless and widows (Deuteronomy 14:28-29). Thus the proportion was clearly specified and every Israelite was obligated to bring to the Lord approximately 22 percent of his yearly income. In contrast, the New Testament merely says "as God hath prospered him." This may mean 8, 12, 20, 50 percent—any percent, depending on the individual case. It may also mean a variation in proportion from year to year, for there is no reason to believe that the proportion suitable for one year will be satisfactory for the next. When prosperity comes, as it has for many Christians, it should be used to give more, not necessarily to buy more. Each time the Christian gives he is to reflect on God's blessing in his life and determine what proportion in return he will give to God. A variation in the proportion means just this—not an increase or decrease merely in the amount given, but a change in the proportion of one's income which is given to the Lord (which of course will also change the amount).

3. *Giving is to be in private deposit—"lay by him in store."*

Contrary to the usual belief, the Christian is not told to turn his gift into the church treasury each Sunday. The Greek word *in store* means to gather and lay up to heap up, to treasure; and the reflexive pronoun *to himself* indicates that the gift is to be kept in private, not public, deposit. The picture in this verse is clearly of a private gift fund into which the believer places his proportionately determined gifts and out of which he distributes to specific causes. This does not mean that either the giving into such a fund or the paying out from such a fund is spasmodic. Neither does it mean that regular giving or even pledging is contrary to the New Testament principles of giving (cf. II Corinthians 8:10-11 where a pledge was made and where Paul exhorted them to fulfill their pledge). But it does mean that there should be, however small, an ever-ready supply of money available to give out as the Spirit directs.

4. *Giving should be periodic—"on the first day of the week."*

It has already been pointed out that giving is not an erratic business. The laying by in private store should be done on Sunday. The Lord's Day is God's appointed day for keeping accounts, determining proportions, and laying by in store. The Scriptures do not say much about what the Christian should or should not do on Sunday except that he should assemble with other believers in worship (Hebrews 10:25) and do his giving (I Corinthians 16:2). Although one need not become ritualistic about this matter of caring for our giving to the Lord on Sunday, neither should it be treated lightly. Here is a God-given command which we would do well to heed. I have made a practice of doing this, and strange as it may seem, doing it on the Lord's Day seems to bring an added blessing. Often, too, the Lord's Day provides a better time away from the distractions of the duties of the week to think more clearly and carefully about this important matter. One of my students tried this one year and testified to the blessing it brought to his family; for, gathered together as a family group on Sunday afternoon thinking and praying together about their giving to the Lord, their spiritual ties were strengthened. If God has suggested it, it is certainly worth trying.

But, someone will say, why go to all this trouble? Why not just take a tithe out of every paycheck and place it in the collection place the following Sunday? The word *tithe* is found in the New Testament only eight times (Matthew 23:23; Luke 11:42; 18:12; Hebrews 7:5-6, 8-9). In the references in the Gospels it is used in connection with that which the Pharisees were doing in fulfilling their obligation to the Mosaic law. In the references in Hebrews tithing is used to prove the inferiority of the Levitical priesthood to the Melchizedek priesthood. Since Levi paid tithes in Abraham when Abraham met Melchizedek, he demonstrates the recognized superiority of Melchizedek and of his priesthood. The passage does not go on and say (as is often implied) that we Christians, therefore, should pay tithes to Christ our High Priest.

It is apparent that the tithe was part of the Mosaic law (Leviticus 27:30-33) and an important factor in the economy of Israel. The law was never given to Gentiles and is expressly done away for the Christian (Romans 2:14; II Corinthians 3:7-13; Hebrews 7:11-12). Neither are the words of Malachi 3 for the Christian, for what believer claims to be a son of Jacob to whom the passage is addressed (v. 6)? Furthermore, material blessing is never promised today as an automatic reward for faithfulness in any area of Christian living, including giving. Spiritual blessing (Ephesians 1:3) and the meeting of material needs (Philippians 4:19) are what God promises. Being prospered materially is no necessary sign of deep godliness of faithful tithing; and contrariwise, poverty is no indication of being out of God's will (cf. Paul's own case in Philippians 4:12).

But, it may be asked, since tithing was practiced before the law, does not that fact make irrelevant all that has been said above and leave tithing as the proper principle to follow in giving? Since Abraham and Jacob both tithed, and since their acts antedated the law, does that not relieve tithing of its legal aspects and make it a valid principle to follow today? The answer would be yes if there were no other guides for giving in the New Testament. If the New Testament were silent on the matter, then of course we would seek for guidance anywhere we could find it in the Bible; but since the New Testament gives us clear principles to govern our giving, there is no need to go back to two isolated examples in the Old Testament for guidance. The fact that something was done before the law which was later incorporated into the law does not necessarily make that thing a good example for today, especially if the New Testament gives further guidance on the matter. Not even the most ardent tither would say that the Sabbath should be observed today because it was observed before the law (Exodus 16:23-36), yet this is the very reasoning used in promoting tithing today. The New Testament teaches us about a new day of worship, and it also gives us new directions for giving. To tithe today following the examples of those who did it before the law would mean that only 10 percent of one's income would go to the Lord and only on certain occasions; to tithe on the basis of the teaching of the law would mean that 22 percent would be given to the Lord as payment of what was owed Him; but to give on the basis of the principles of the New Testament might mean any percent, and given in recognition that 100 percent belongs to Him. The Lord's work will never lack support if we preach and practice New Testament principles of giving.

Proportionate giving is not starting with a tithe and then doing what more we can when we can. Proportionate giving is giving as God hath prospered. If someone felt after prayer that the right proportion for him should be 10 percent, I would suggest that he give 9 or 11 percent just to keep out of the 10 percent rut. A person who is giving 9 or 11 percent will find himself much more sensitive to the Lord's changing his proportion than if he were giving 10 percent.

Every believer owes 100 percent of what he is and what he has to God. The question, then, is not only how much I give, but also how much I spend on myself. Proportionate giving alone can furnish the right answer to this matter and for every stage of life. We give because He gave, not because He commanded; we give because we want to, not because we have to; we give because we love Him, and we show that love most concretely in this way. If in turn God blesses us materially, we praise Him; if not, we still praise Him. This is grace giving, and this is the proof of our love for God.

Years ago Lewis Sperry Chafer wrote some choice words on the subject "Spirit-directed Giving." He defined this as "depending only on the Spirit of God to direct the gifts in the case of every person, and then being willing to abide by the results of this confidence and trust." Although not denying the need to be well informed about needs, he expressed the fear that "too many of our churches have been trained to respond only to the insistent human appeal, and this, like some medicine, requires an ever-increasing dose to produce the desired effect." Practicing this principle of information without solicitation, D. M. Stearns used to read to his congregation messages from Christian workers and then instruct his people to withhold their gifts unless not to give would burden their souls. "How jealously the giver should guard against any and all forms of human pressure which might mislead him away from the discharge of his God-given responsibility, which responsibility is to find and to do the precise will of God! ... Is your giving in obedience to the still, small voice of the Spirit of God? Are you, too, a part of the great divine faith system?" This is grace giving, because it is Spirit-directed giving, and it is one of the most blessed experiences a believer may have.

BUYING

But giving is only half the story of money and our love for God. If everything comes from the Lord and belongs to Him, and if we have dedicated ourselves to Him, then not only is what we give to Him important but also what we spend on ourselves is indicative of our love. It is fallacious reasoning to think that when we have given a portion of our income to the Lord the rest belongs to us. It is all His; we merely use part of it for ourselves.

Although the average family's income is up considerably from what it was a few years ago, the universal complaint is "I do not have enough money." Everyone seems to want more, which, of course, is not wrong in itself. One wonders, however, for what purpose people want more money. It seems that very few have this goal in order to be able to increase their giving to the Lord's work. When all things are considered the purpose in too many cases seems to be to have more things. Today, the abundant economic life has become the necessary life for the American society.

But, someone may be thinking, what is wrong with having more material goods? What is so evil about the luxuries of the past generation becoming the necessities of this present generation? Is that not progress? And does not God want us to enjoy all things? After all, the Bible does not condemn things—just the love of things.

Unquestionably, the Christian's use of money is the object of pulls and pressures from every side, whether it be from the advertising industry, from our own desires, or from the world around us. Every child of God needs help in discovering what is right and what is wrong in the use of money, particularly in an age of prosperity and full employment. If times were hard and money were tight, many of the problems would automatically disappear. It is an often overlooked truism that it is easier to live by faith when you do *not* have any money than when you do. After all, when you have nothing, you have little choice about how to live. You are much more inclined, if not actually forced, to live in total dependence on the Lord. But when you have money in the bank, you have a choice. You can spend it by faith, or you can spend it directed by self. Thus in a situation of plenty, it becomes most important to use properly the wealth that God gives us.

What does the Bible say about the use of money? Are luxuries worldly? May I have a new car, even a big car, in the will of God, for instance? Of course, the Bible does not say whether so many particular things are right or wrong to buy and have. But the Scriptures do give some plain principles that should govern the use of all money, for God is not simply concerned with the percent we give to Him but with 100 percent of what we possess.

The passage of Scripture which gives us these principles is seldom thought of when money is mentioned; it is I Timothy 6. An interesting feature of I Timothy is the connection between false teachers and money. And yet it is not a surprising connection, for false teachers usually are selfish in their desire for money, and false doctrine will affect the proper use of money as quickly as any aspect of living. An unscriptural attitude toward money is a great spiritual peril.

In contrast to the teaching of the false teachers, Paul's overall governing principle in regard to wealth is this: "Godliness with contentment is great gain" (I Timothy 6:6). Great gain does not necessarily come from two cars in the garage, but it comes from godliness and contentment. This word *gain* means "basic necessities." Godliness with contentment is the basic necessity of the Christian's life. No matter what else a man has, unless he has this, he has only a superstructure without a foundation.

What is godliness? It includes at least what Paul describes in verse 11 as righteousness, faith, love, patience and meekness. Contentment includes those inner resources placed in the believer's life by grace, which will make him contented within the varying moods and circumstances of life. It is the contentment of knowing "how to be abased, and ... how to abound" (Philippians 4:12). This does not mean that a man should not try to improve his lot in life, but it does mean that contentment involves learning to love the will of God regardless of the circumstances into which it may bring a person. In want content, and in plenty content—remembering that it is sometimes more difficult to be content in plenty than in want. This is the first great principle to guide the believer through the maze of the abundant life.

In terms of everyday living, this principle means, among other things, that the acquisition of the latest gadgets is not the most important matter in life. The believer who is not thus surrounded with the latest of everything should not be frustrated even if neighbors and other Christians look on the outward appearance, for God still looks on the heart. In His children's hearts the Lord wants first of all to find godliness with contentment. Buying too much may be a demonstration of our love for things and a proof of our lack of love for God.

Lest anyone think that this principle justifies idling in pious meditation all day without giving attention to financial responsibilities, Paul makes it abundantly clear that the Christian is obliged to support his minister (I Timothy 5:17-18) and his family (5:8). Failing to do this is to class oneself worse than an infidel.

Another great principle in this chapter is this: Do not love money or what it can buy. "For the love of money is the root of all evil" (6:10). On the one hand it means that the Christian must not covet money or the things it can buy. On the other hand, the injunction does not say that the Christian should not enjoy the things that God gives him if they are placed in proper perspective and bought in the will of God. Important, too, is the fact that this verse does not say that money itself is evil but only that one's attitude toward it may be evil. Indeed, Paul says in this very chapter that God has given us all things to enjoy (v. 17). Some fraudulently pious people are proud or falsely humble over what they do not have! No false humility or even sense of shame is warranted if *God* gives you something. And if it is something new in the will of God, be thankful, enjoy it, and do not be ashamed of having something nice and new. On the other hand, if last year's model has to do when other Christians have the latest, let godliness with contentment, not the love of things, rule the heart. It is important, too, to remember that getting something at a discount does not necessarily make it right. Things can be wrong at any price.

Of course, many "things" are without moral character in themselves. It is the believer's attitude toward things and not the things themselves that constitutes good or evil. An automobile is not evil. A new car is not evil. The *best model* of a new car is not evil. But the cheapest used car may be flagrantly evil for the Christian already staggered by debts and stingy about his giving to God. The world system leaves God out; thus any purchase that leaves God out is a flirtation with the world system. Logic: "It was such a good deal"; rationalization: "But it was on sale" are not justifications for buying anything or spending any money outside of the will of God.

Thus a doctrine of how to buy and prove our love for God in any economic situation is basically this: (1) Learn contentment in the will of God in every circumstance of life; and (2) love God more than any "thing" either possessed or desired. When prosperity comes as it has for many believers, the spiritual Christian will use it to give more (in proportion, not merely in dollar amount), not necessarily to buy more.

Paul concludes this chapter of principles for personal finances with this reminder (and remember that these words do not apply just to those who are in a higher income bracket—they apply to most Christians today): "Charge them that are rich in this world, that they be not high-minded, nor trust in uncertain riches, but in the living God, who giveth us richly all things to enjoy; that they do good, that they be rich in good works, ready to distribute, willing to communicate; laying up in store for themselves a good foundation against the time to come, that they may lay hold on eternal life" (I Timothy 6:17-19).

A spiritual Christian will practice full giving in full employment, inflated giving in an inflated economy, and careful buying at all times. And by his use of all his money he will prove or disprove his love for God.

CHAPTER 10

HOW TO FACE THE DEATH OF A LOVED ONE

ELISABETH ELLIOT

IT'S GONE. I COULD SEE the yellow-spoked wheel of the spare tire, perched on the back of a 1934 Plymouth, disappear over the hilltop. The car in which I might have got a ride home from elementary school on this rainy day had gone and I was left behind.

"It's gone." The trainman stood at the only lighted gate in Penn Station. The train had gone, leaving me behind to figure out how on earth I was to make a speaking engagement on Long Island in an hour and a half.

We've all experienced the desolation of being left in one way or another. And sooner or later many of us experience the greatest desolation of all: he's gone. The one who made life what it was for us, who was, in fact, our life.

And we were not ready. Not really prepared at all. We felt, when the fact stared us in the face, "No. Not yet." For however bravely we may have looked at the possibilities (if we had any warning at all), however calmly we may have

---

Copyright 1973, by CHRISTIANITY TODAY, used by permission.

talked about them with the one who was about to die (and I had a chance to talk about the high risks with my first husband, and about the human hopelessness of the situation with my second), we are caught short. If we had another week, perhaps, to brace ourselves. A few more days to say what we wanted to say, to do or undo some things, wouldn't it have been better, easier?

But silent, swift, and implacable the Scythe has swept by, and he is gone, and we are left. We stand bewildered on the sidewalk, on the station platform. Yet, most strangely, that stunning snatching away has changed nothing very much. There is the sunlight lying in patches on the familiar carpet just as it did yesterday. The same dishes stand in the rack to be put away as usual, his razor and comb are on the shelf, his shoes in the closet (O the shoes! molded in the always recognizable shape of his feet). The mail comes, the phone rings, Wednesday gives way to Thursday and this week to next week, and you have to keep getting up in the morning ("Life must go on, I forget just why," wrote Edna St. Vincent Millay) and combing your hair (for whom, now?), eating breakfast (remember to get out only one egg now, not three), making the bed (who cares?). You have to meet people who most fervently wish they could pass by on the other side so as not to have to think of something to say. You have to be understanding with *their* attempts to be understanding, and when they nervously try to steer you away from the one topic you want so desperately to talk about you have to allow yourself to be steered away—for their sakes. You resist the temptation, when they say he's "passed away," to say "No, he's *dead*, you know."

After a few months you've learned those initial lessons. You begin to say "I" instead of "we" and people have sent their cards and flowers and said the things they ought to say and their lives are going on and so, astonishingly, is yours and you've "adjusted" to some of the differences—as if that little mechanical word, a mere tinkering with your routines and emotions, covers the ascent from the pit.

I speak of the "ascent." I am convinced that every death, of whatever kind, through which we are called to go, must lead to a resurrection. This is the core of Christian faith. Death is the end of every life and leads to resurrection, the beginning of every new one. It is a progression, a proper progression, the way things were meant to be, the necessary means of ongoing life. It is supremely important that every bereaved person be helped to see this. The death of the beloved was the beloved's own death, "a very private personal matter," Gert Behanna says, "and nobody should ever dare to try to get in on the act." But the death of the beloved is also the lover's death, for it means, in a different but perhaps equally fearsome way, a going through the Valley of the Shadow.

I can think of six simple things that have helped me through this valley and that help me now.

First, I try to be still and know that He is God. That advice comes from Psalm 46, which begins by describing the sort of trouble from which God is our refuge—the earth's changing, or "giving way" as the Jerusalem Bible puts it, the mountains shaking, the waters roaring and foaming, nations raging, kingdoms tottering, the earth melting. None of these cataclysms seem an exaggeration of what happens when somebody dies. The things that seemed most dependable have given way altogether. The whole world has a different look and you find it hard to get your bearings. Shadows can be very confusing. But in both psalms we are reminded of one rock-solid fact that nothing can change: Thou art with me. The Lord of Hosts is with us, the God of Jacob is our refuge. We feel that we are alone, yet we are not alone. Not for one moment has He left us alone. He is the one who has "wrought desolations," to be sure. He makes wars cease, breaks bows, shatters spears, burns chariots (breaks hearts, shatters lives?), but in the midst of all this hullabaloo we are commanded, "*Be still.*" Be still and know.

Stillness is something the bereaved may feel they have

entirely too much of. But if they will use that stillness to take a long look at Christ, to listen attentively to His voice, they will get their bearings.

There are several ways of looking and listening that help us avoid being dangerously at the mercy of our (heaven forfend!) "gut-level" feelings. Bible reading and prayer are the obvious ones. Taking yourself by the scruff of the neck and setting aside a definite time in a definite place for deliberately looking at what God has said and listening to what He may have to say to you today is a good exercise. And if such exercises are seen as an obligation, they have the same power other obligations—cooking a meal, cleaning a bathroom, vacuuming a rug—have to save us from ourselves.

Another means of grace is repeating the creed. Here is a list of objective facts that have not been in the smallest detail altered by what has happened to us. Far from it. Not only have they not been altered; they do actually alter what has happened—alter our whole understanding of human life and death, lift it to another plane. We can go through the list and contemplate our situation in the light of each tremendous truth. It is simply amazing how different my situation can appear as a result of this discipline.

The second thing I try to do is to give thanks. I cannot thank God for the murder of one or the excruciating disintegration of another, but I can thank God for the promise of His presence. I can thank Him that He is still in charge, in the face of life's worst terrors, and that "this slight momentary affliction is preparing for us [not 'us for'] an eternal weight of glory beyond all comparison, because we look not to the things that are seen but to the things that are unseen." I'm back to the creed again and the things unseen that are listed there, standing solidly (yes, solidly, incredible as it seems) against things seen (the fact of death, my own loneliness, this empty room). And I am lifted up by the promise of that "weight" of glory, so far greater than the weight of sorrow that at times seems to grind me like a millstone. This promise enables me to give thanks.

Then I try to refuse self-pity. I know of nothing more paralyzing, more deadly, than self-pity. It is a death that has no resurrection, a sink-hole from which no rescuing hand can drag you because you have chosen to sink. But it must be refused. In order to refuse it, of course, I must recognize it for what it is. Amy Carmichael, in her sword-thrust of a book *If*, wrote, "If I make much of anything appointed, magnify it secretly to myself or insidiously to others, then I know nothing of Calvary love." That's a good definition of self-pity—making much of the "appointed," magnifying it, dwelling on one's own losses, looking with envy on those who appear to be more fortunate than oneself, asking "why me, Lord?" (remembering the "weight of glory" ought to be a sufficient answer to that question). It is one thing to call a spade a spade, to acknowledge that this thing is indeed suffering. It's no use telling yourself it's nothing. When Paul called it a "slight" affliction he meant it only by comparison with the glory. But it's another thing to regard one's own suffering as uncommon, or disproportionate, or undeserved. What have "deserts" got to do with anything? We are all under the Mercy, and Christ knows the precise weight and proportion of our sufferings—*He bore them.* He carried our sorrows. He suffered, wrote George Macdonald, not that we might not suffer, but that our sufferings might be like His. To hell, then, with self-pity.

The next thing to do is to accept my loneliness. When God takes a loved person from my life it is in order to call me, in a new way, to Himself. It is therefore a vocation. It is in this sphere, for now, anyway, that I am to learn of him. Every stage on the pilgrimage is a chance to know him, to be brought to him. Loneliness is a stage (and, thank God, only a stage) when we are terribly aware of our own helplessness. It "opens the gates of my soul," wrote Katherine Mansfield, "and lets the wild beasts stream howling through." We may accept this, thankful that it brings us to the Very Present Help.

The acceptance of loneliness can be followed immediately by the offering of it up to God. Something mysterious and miraculous transpires as soon as something is held up in our hands as a gift. He takes it from us, as Jesus took the little lunch when five thousand people were hungry. He gives thanks for it and then, breaking it, transforms it for the good of others. Loneliness looks pretty paltry as a gift to offer to God—but then when you come to think of it so does anything else we might offer. It needs transforming. Others looking at it would say exactly what the disciples said, "What's the good of that with such a crowd?" But it was none of their business what use the Son of God would make of it. And it is none of ours. It is ours only to give it.

The last of the helps I have found is to do something for somebody else. There is nothing like definite, overt action to overcome the inertia of grief. The appearance of Joseph of Arimathea to take away the body of Jesus must have greatly heartened the other disciples, so prostrate with their own grief that they had probably not thought of doing anything at all. Nicodemus, too, thought of something he could do—he brought a mixture of myrrh and aloes—and the women who had come with Jesus from Galilee went off to prepare spices and ointments. This clear-cut action lifted them out of themselves. That is what we need in a time of crisis. An old piece of wisdom is "Doe the next thynge." Most of us have someone who needs us. If we haven't, we can find someone. Instead of praying only for the strength we ourselves need to survive, this day or this hour, how about praying for some to give away? How about trusting God to fulfill His own promise, "My strength is made perfect in weakness"? Where else is His strength more perfectly manifested than in a human being who, well knowing his own weakness, lays hold by faith on the Strong Son of God, Immortal Love?

It is here that a great spiritual principle goes into

operation. Isaiah 58:10-12 says, "If you pour yourself out for the hungry and satisfy the desire of the afflicted, then shall your light rise in the darkness and your gloom be as the noonday. And the Lord will guide you continually and satisfy your desire with good things, and make your bones strong; and you shall be like a watered garden, like a spring of water, whose waters fail not, and ... you shall be called a repairer of the breach, the restorer of streets to dwell in [or, in another translation, 'paths leading home']."

The condition on which all these wonderful gifts (light, guidance, satisfaction, strength, refreshment to others) rests is an unexpected one—unexpected, that is, if we are accustomed to think in material instead of in spiritual terms. The condition is not that one solve his own problems first. He need not "get it together." The condition is simply "if you pour yourself out."

Countless others have found this to work. St. Francis of Assisi put the principle into other words in his great prayer, "Lord, make me an instrument of thy peace. Where there is darkness let me sow light, where there is sadness, joy.... Grant that I may not so much seek to be consoled as to console.... For it is in giving that we receive; it is in pardoning that we are pardoned; it is in dying that we are born to eternal life." The words of this prayer were like a light to me in the nights of my husband's last illness, and I wondered then at the marvel of a man's prayer being answered (was I the millionth to be blessed by it?) some seven hundred years after he had prayed it. St. Francis was most certainly during those nights in 1973 an instrument of God's peace.

Perhaps it is peace, of all God's earthly gifts, that in our extremity we long for most. A priest told me of a terminally ill woman who asked him each time he came to visit only to pray, "The peace of God which passeth all understanding keep your hearts and minds through Christ Jesus."

I have often prayed, in thinking of the many bereaved, the

words of the beautiful hymn "Sun of my Soul":

> Be every mourner's sleep tonight
> Like infant slumbers, pure and bright.

There they are—six things that, if done in faith, can be the way to resurrection: be still and know, give thanks, refuse self-pity, accept the loneliness, offer it to God, turn your energies toward the satisfaction not of your own needs but of others'. And there will be no calculating the extent to which

> From the ground there blossoms red
> Life that shall endless be.

CHAPTER 11

HOW TO OVERCOME THE TIME TRAP

BOB SHEFFIELD

THE "TIME TRAP" IS familiar to all of us. How do we use what little "free" time we have in the most profitable manner? If after meeting all the demands of husband, wife, parent, provider, etc., I only have a few hours a week to invest in others, what activities should I choose?

In recent months I have faced this dilemma personally. My job as a Navigator demands a certain amount of travel and being away from home. Then when I'm home I must catch up on office work and preparations for future ministry. However, I still feel the need to have a personal ministry not as a Navigator but as a Christian.

Nancy and I decided to invest time with five couples back in August. We had prayed and God indicated we should give ourselves to these five. But, like you, we faced the "time problem." As we thought, it became apparent that the morning was a good time for the men to meet. So at 6:30 a.m. on Monday and Friday mornings we meet for prayer, study,

---

Reprinted by permission of The Navigators.

and sharing. I can't begin to enumerate the things that have happened to us and these men in three months.

We meet as couples every other week for an in-depth Bible study. This is an all evening affair. It begins at 7:30 and usually we have to encourage the last couple to leave well after 11:00 p.m. Again it is impossible to write about all that God is doing in each life through the study of His Word. In the beginning I thought it would be up to me to lead and teach, however that is not so. The Holy Spirit is teaching each participant and I have been on the receiving end.

Recently we decided to have an evangelistic dessert and each of the five couples invited some friends. Our purpose was to provide an activity which would allow us to expose our non-church friends to what we had found meaningful in life. That is first a personal relationship with Christ and then growth with others through individual Bible study plus group sharing. From this activity at least two couples are now actively studying about the Savior!

Now let me summarize what I have tried to expose you to! First of all there are tremendous demands on our time. We must evaluate our schedule and learn to live by priorities. Ask yourself this question. What will be the lasting results of this activity in light of eternity? Stated another way, five years from now will what I'm involved in have any lasting fruit?

Secondly, we can have a significant impact with little investment if we really desire it. For instance to get up two mornings a week and meet with these men has paid fantastic dividends. I computed the total time spent with these men and their wives to be less than twenty hours per month. For the time spent this investment is paying premium benefits.

Thirdly, it is not difficult to start. All of us have friends who really want to grow and develop spiritually. We just need the courage to ask God to give us the right ones to begin with and then begin! There is no end to the helps available in terms of materials. Any Christian bookstore has numerous studies and books available. Or write to our headquarters for a catalog of resources.

Fourth, remember that no group survives if it is totally introspective. With intake there must be output or else we will stagnate. Our objective with these couples is two-fold: "To know Christ and to make Him known." If our meeting together does not have a mission or outreach it soon loses its dynamic.

I hope these thoughts have been helpful. I'm excited because Nancy and I have now realized that we can overcome the time trap if we keep our priorities straight.... "And we proclaim Him, admonishing every man and teaching every man with all wisdom, that we may present every man complete in Christ. And for this purpose also I labor, striving according to His power, which mightily works within me" (Colossians 1:28, 29 NASB).

CHAPTER 12

HOW TO ACT LIKE A CHRISTIAN

L. NELSON BELL

"THE CHURCH SPENDS much of its time trying to make non-Christians act like Christians." This is an observation I have stated and written a number of times, and I think it is true. But once when I said it in a group of ministers, men honestly and earnestly preaching the Gospel, one godly pastor observed: "My problem is trying to get *Christians* to act like Christians."

Sober thought reveals how true this is in our own lives, and in the lives of other Christians. How few of us act as Christians should act! How frequently our actions and reactions are unloving! How often we belie our Christian profession by word and deed!

People become Christians through faith in Jesus Christ and in no other way. It is impossible to do *anything* that will bring us into a right relationship with God. This has been done for us and must be received by faith.

Nevertheless, living as one of the redeemed is a matter of

Copyright 1976, by CHRISTIANITY TODAY, used by permission.

growing in grace and involves an act of the will, a will enlightened, motivated, and empowered by the Holy Spirit.

Living as a Christian means exhibiting many facets of God's grace in our hearts, all of them the outgrowth of Christian love and all of them polished and brightened by practice. These graces are the outward expression of an inner Presence and attitude, the putting into practice of those things we know are good and right.

Sympathy. There is hardly a day that we do not come in contact with someone who has been buffeted by the winds of adversity. All around us there are those who sorrow, who are suffering from illness, poverty, despair, bereavement.

How utterly un-Christian to be indifferent toward this suffering. True sympathy is begotten by love and expressed at the personal level. The Christian, having experienced the comfort of the Holy Spirit, should know how to sympathize with others.

Speaking of this the Apostle Paul says: "[God] comforteth us in all our tribulation, that we may be able to comfort them which are in any trouble, by the comfort wherewith we ourselves are comforted of God" (II Corinthians 1:4).

Compassion. There is a distinction between sympathy and compassion, for compassion involves depth of understanding—one sinner's being sorry for another sinner's plight.

Compassion looks deep into the heart, suffers with and understands the need of the other person, and communicates that understanding. Compassion ignores the unlovely as it sees God's image in most unlikely places.

Courtesy. Courtesy is the art and grace of treating others with respect and understanding—just as we would like to be treated. It is politeness in the face of provocation, the turning of the other cheek when we have been offended.

Courtesy involves the soft answer that can turn away wrath. It is observance of the niceties of social intercourse in the midst of trying circumstances.

Only too often unhappy situations develop because of the lack of common courtesy. That this should be true where Christians are concerned is a travesty, reflecting dishonor on the very name Christian.

Patience. Impatience has dimmed the witness of many a Christian. How often we must distress our Lord by our impatience with others. Some people seem slow, inarticulate, and inept—just the way we appear to our Lord, perhaps. And he is infinitely patient with us.

Tact. Frankness is not always for the glory of God. I have known some Christians who have prided themselves on being frank, and I have known some who have been hurt by this frankness. Telling the truth can be done in love, taking into consideration the feelings of others. There is a vast difference in the remarks of two shoe salesmen, one of whom said, "I'm sorry, madam, but your foot is too big for this shoe," while the other said, "I am sorry, but this shoe is too small for you."

Tact is that grace which enables us to sense the feelings of others and to act toward them or communicate with them in a way that preserves human dignity.

Forgiveness. Without a spirit of forgiveness, human relations cannot be maintained at the Christian level. We live in the light of God's forgiveness, and it is an attitude that God *requires* of us. Forgiveness involves shedding the robe of self-righteousness and being clothed with the humility that is a part of true Christianity.

Practicality. We often are sound in theory but fail at the point of implementation. To many of us the Christian graces are nebulous attributes that we expect in others but fail to exhibit ourselves.

Practicality involves helping people in the place where they need help. It is not just a kind word but also a kind act where that act can do the most good. Where food is needed, give food. Where clothing is needed, give clothing. Where comfort, sympathy, courtesy, and patience are needed, show these. The Apostle James admonishes us: "Be ye doers of the word, and not hearers only, deceiving your own selves." Acting like a Christian means just that.

In these things the Christian must rigorously search his own heart, at the same time determining by God's help to grow in those aspects of grace that so intimately affect others, while they reflect Christ in our own hearts.

C. S. Lewis has well said, "Do not waste your time bothering whether you 'love' your neighbor or not; act as if you did. As soon as you do this you find one of the great secrets. When you are behaving as if you loved someone, you will presently come to love him."

The exhibiting of the grace of God in our dealings with others must be for the glory of God. Unbelievers see Christ through the lives of Christians—and what a sorry spectacle is often paraded before them!

The exhibiting of Christian graces is a matter of practice, of growing, and of outward witnessing. In this the effectiveness of our salvation is exhibited to others. When we fail to act like Christians, we dishonor the One whose name we bear.

The world needs the evidence of sanctification in the Christian's life. This is evidence of the power of God to redeem and change, and also a balm to a sin-sick world.

CHAPTER 13

HOW TO GET ALONG WITH OTHER CHRISTIANS
ROBERT WEBBER

DOES ANYONE CHOOSE to be poor? Yes—not only monks but some protestants too. In recent years pockets of Christians who have gotten serious about following the Master have taken literally His words to the rich young ruler, "If thou wilt be perfect, go and sell what thou hast, and give to the poor, and thou shalt have treasure in heaven; and come follow me" (Matthew 19:21).

Is poverty *the* Christian way? Yes, said a majority of my colleagues during a recent conference in Chicago for evangelical Christians. Specifically an American Christian ought to live on $2,000 a year, they argued. It is the only way to forcibly demonstrate the triumph of God over mammon.

Several of us wondered about allowances for New York City versus, say, rural Indiana with a two-acre garden out back—or living alone versus in a family of five (which would have $10,000 aggregate), or even a common-purse community.

Reprinted by permission of THE OTHER SIDE, Box 158, Savannah, Ohio 44874.

But our questions were easy compared to those of one gentleman, a businessman who not only owned a new home, but a boat and a Mercedes Benz besides. He was attempting to be a serious Christian as well; last year he had given away $35,000 (more than one-third of his income). "What am I to do?" he asked. "I simply cannot cut back to $2,000 a year. If I sell out to a non-Christian, he probably won't give what I am giving to the Lord's work. Can you accept me as I am and consider me a true disciples of Jesus?"

Several said yes. Others courteously but adamantly insisted that he should change, arguing that the choice of personal poverty is a mark of real discipleship.

I thought as I listened to the committee's debate that Menno Simons would be proud of this new revival of Anabaptist thought. Anabaptists emerged in the sixteenth century as what has been dubbed "the left wing of the Reformation." Their chief concern was that the reform of Luther in Germany and Zwingli in Zurich had not gone far enough. For them, Luther and Zwingli (and later Calvin) had reformed only the medieval church. They had rid the church of *some* of its false practices and errors but not *all*. Anabaptists sought to restore the church to its original simplicity, poverty, and purity as demonstrated in the New Testament and the pre-Constantinian era.

They saw a difference between the message of Jesus and the message about Jesus. For them, Jesus' message emphasizes "Follow me," whereas the disciples' message appears to emphasize "Believe in Jesus." There is, the Anabaptist would argue, a direct relationship between one's understanding of the faith and one's wealth. The person who understands faith in terms of discipleship will be led to a radical rejection of possessions, whereas one who identifies faith with belief is more prone to be accepting of affluence.

In their view, the church from Constantine on emphasized belief in Jesus whereas the early church (100-311) and the Anabaptist church of the sixteenth century emphasized the message of Jesus: "Follow me." For them, mere belief in Jesus is too easy, too undemanding. But Anabaptists, who also believe, are mainly concerned about discipleship, about living out the kingdom principles. They see life in terms of two kingdoms which are totally separate from each other. One is the kingdom of Satan, the other is the kingdom of God. The kingdom of Satan is the culture of this world. The kingdom of God is the culture of the church, the pure body of visible saints on this earth. The heart of the matter is captured in the word *separation*. There is a separation between the two kingdoms. The unregenerate belong in one; the regenerate in the other.

For this reason, Anabaptists tend toward community. The community is the pure church, a group of Christians who live their whole lives under the standard of the heavenly kingdom taught by Jesus, particularly in the Sermon on the Mount. This community which represents the kingdom of God on earth is expressed in Communities ranging all the way from a very separtistic Hutterite or Amish community to a less separtistic Mennonite community, or a group like Reba Place Fellowship or other modern communal living centers.

Now our business man, according to the Anabaptist position, is wrong. Wealth and power belong to the kingdom of the world order. Therefore, a Christian has no right involving himself in a worldly system when his whole life is to be lived out under the kingdom rule, in separation from the rule of Satan in the world. He has no choice but to give up his job, sell his possessions, give away his money, and live by Jesus' teaching on poverty.

But there in the committee room, I found myself wondering whether Luther could not have shed some light on the problem as well as the Anabaptists. If Luther had been there, he too would have begun talking about two kingdoms, but he would have meant something very different. Mankind, according to Martin Luther, is divided into those who belong to the kingdom of God and all those who belong to the kingdom of this world.

The kingdom of this world is earthy, and its functions is to preserve life. It is the rule which God, through creation, has given to man, over everything that is earthly. Man is to function as God's steward over business and secular government, in marriage and the family, in education and art. Man's rule in the kingdom of this world is his function as a creature of God over the total creation of God.

On the other hand, the kingdom of God is the spiritual kingdom of Christ, His rule in the heart of the man justified by faith, and His rule in the life of the church.

Both of these kingdoms are under the sovereign rule of God. The kingdom of the world is under God by virtue of creation and is to be ruled by the laws of creation and God's revealed moral law. In this kingdom, man is to rule by justice with retribution and punishment for evil. But the kingdom of God is under God by virtue of redemption. God rules in this kingdom through love and forgiveness mediated by His spirit. At face value, then, everything in both kingdoms belongs to God. All of life is good and to be enjoyed because God is the creator. Man is therefore free to enjoy the wealth of creation (not just possessions) because God has declared all things good and lawful for all men.

But Satan is the great spoiler. Because Satan has caused man to sin, man tends to worship the creature (or some aspect of the created order) rather than the Creator. Therefore, man misuses that which is good, and his misuse of things—not the things themselves—is evil. Thus when wealth or abundance, which in and of themselves are good, are made the central desire of a person's life, they become gods and therefore evil.

The Christian now living in the world finds himself in an awkward tension between the culture of the kingdom of this world, which because of evil misuses God's good creation and mismanages God's government over this world, and the kingdom of God, which has different standards such as love, forgiveness, and non-attachment to the goods of this world. Because the Christian has a dual existence, in the world and in Christ, this tension necessarily results in a compromise.

Luther could make a good case for our wealthy business man who makes his money in the kingdom of this world. Luther would point out that this gentleman is simply experiencing the tension between the kingdom of the world and the kingdom of God. He wears two hats. He operates in two worlds, so to speak. Consequently the ideal which he holds to in the kingdom of God cannot be fully and completely realized in the kingdom of the world. He has no choice, Luther would say, but to "sin boldly." That is, he should do his work in the world boldly because life has been spoiled by Satan, and the perfect kingdom will not be realized until Christ's return. So, in the meantime he is to go about his work with a sense of vocation (calling from God) which sensitizes him toward his responsibility. Luther would say that our business man is doing the right thing. He is doing his job well and giving a handsome proportion to the work of the Lord.

And what about Calvin, I thought. Suppose he were here: would not he have even a third way of looking at this problem?

Calvin, like Augustine, builds on the creation-sin-redemption triad. He goes back to the covenant of works between God and man in the garden. In this covenant, man had both a moral and a cultural responsibility. Morally he was to keep God's command not to eat of the Tree of the Knowledge of Good and Evil. Culturally, he was to dress and keep the garden, name the animals, and subdue the earth. In other words, he was given a mandate to unfold culture under God. In obedience to God, man had the potential to develop a culture that in every way showed forth God's beauty and design in a truly religious civilization.

But because of sin, man became morally depraved,

disobedient to God's will, and self-centered. Consequently, he unfolded culture in keeping with his sinful nature. Civilization was soon full of wickedness and sin, not only in the moral and personal sense, but also in a corporate sense. The order of the world deteriorated into violence, greed, corruption and injustice. In the world men hate and cheat each other, kings and governments rule without respect to fairness, equality and justice. Nations war over land and oil and ideologies. In other words, Satan rules in culture, because he rules in the hearts of men who unfold culture.

But in Jesus Christ a new order has broken into the world. A redemption, a release from the hold that Satan has over the hearts of men has taken place. Satan is no longer lord and master; Christ is now the Lord over all of life. This Lordship of Christ extends over man's moral, spiritual and cultural life. Now man has a new awareness of his cultural responsibility; he is to unfold culture according to God's design, which puts him in radical antithesis to the design of Satan. Thus, for Calvinists, the key word describing man's cultural responsibility is *conversion.* He is called under God to convert, to change, to redirect the structures of life according to the design and plan of God.

Take our business man, for example. The Calvinist would agree with the Lutheran that he could be in business, make his money in a corrupt culture, and give a good portion to needy causes. But the Calvinist would show a greater concern toward changing the structure. The Calvinist, less prone to dismiss the evils of the economic order as a consequence of a realistic tension that permeates culture, would be involved in unions and other active organizations insisting on changes in corporate structures to bring them into closer conformity to God's desire for justice, righteousness, and love toward persons, and care and respect for His creation.

Our group didn't resolve the issue; it ended up calling rather equivocally for personal and corporate responsibility in all economic matters. To be truthful, I'm not sure that we can resolve the question by siding either with the Anabaptists, with Luther, or with Calvin. *It seems to me that each position contains part of the truth and not the whole, and that the three positions taken together give us greater insight into the truth than any one alone.*

If that is so, then, there are some important facts that emerge out of these three models on which we can all agree. Let me suggest what they are:

  1. *There is a fundamental dualism about reality.* This is not a dualism between God and the world, spirit and matter, sacred and secular, as though some of life is good and some is not. Instead, it is the dualism of two rules within God's creation—the rule of Satan and the rule of Christ.

  2. *A Christian view of life must take this basic dualism in life seriously.* That is, it must be recognized that in every aspect of life—cultural, spiritual, moral, political, etc.—we "wrestle not against flesh and blood, but against the principalities, against the powers, against the world rulers of this present darkness, against the spiritual hosts of wickedness in the heavenly places" (Eph. 6:12).

  3. *Therefore, the proper Christian response to the world is multiform:* (a) The Christian needs to be *separate* from the world. Paul urges Christians in Rome not to be "conformed to this world but be transformed by the renewal of your mind" (Romans 12:2). Certainly no Christian can allow himself to be ruled by the ideologies of the world; some, in order to demonstrate the wickedness of the world mind-set, will choose to physically separate themselves from the world through communal living. (b) Yet the Christian inevitably participates in the world. Paul realizes that the conflicting needs of separation and participation cause tension when he writes "for I do not do the good I want, but the evil I do not want is what I do" (Romans 7:19). Even the most radical Hutterite is still a part of this world order, and to some extent a participant in it. To a degree, we all compromise our

convictions, because the kingdom of God will not be fully realized unto Christ's second coming. (c) The Christian is also commanded to *convert* culture. Amos makes it very clear that God wants "justice to roll down like waters, and righteousness like an ever-flowing stream" (Amos 5:24). Surely we all agree that part of our Christian witness is to bring the character of God to bear on societal structures.

4. *No person or group can make these three responses in a totally balanced way.* For that reason some Christians are called to emphasize one approach more than the other. Therefore,

5. *The truth of the Christian's relation to culture is demonstrated more clearly by the whole than any part.* Thus,

6. *We need each other.*

Now let's go back again to our business man. If we take the approach I've suggested above, then our business man becomes an accepted part of the body of Christ, encouraged by all the various manifestations of Christ's body to be responsible with his life, particularly with his money.

Christians today face an exciting and open future. For this reason, we have a great responsibility not to repeat the mistakes of the past, particularly not to be devisive, to create unnecessary enemies, or to cut off from fellowship other members of the body of Christ who don't see things quite our way.

Furthermore, we have a responsibility to break through establishment notions, to cut a new path into the future for evangelical Christians. If we divide the Church and sling mud at those who do not agree with us, we will fail—and deservedly so. But I believe God is calling us to a new kind of responsibility, a responsibility which sees the Church of Jesus Christ as *one*, going about its task in the world. I believe we can accept this new leadership only after we learn to accept each other as necessary to the body of Christ. May God grant us this unity!

CHAPTER 14

HOW TO DEEPEN CHURCH LIFE THROUGH SMALL GROUPS

HOWARD A. SNYDER

A SMALL GROUP OF eight to twelve people meeting together informally in homes is the most effective structure for the communication of the gospel in modern secular-urban society. Such groups are better suited to the mission of the church in today's urban world than are traditional church services, institutional church programs, or the mass communication media. Methodologically speaking, the small group offers the best hope for revival and renewal within the church.

Let me explain my reasons for these conclusions.

The small group was the basic unit of the church's life during its first two centuries. There were no church buildings then; Christians met almost exclusively in private homes (and seldom, as we usually think, in the catacombs). In fact, the use of small groups of one kind or another seems to be a common element in all significant movements of the Holy Spirit throughout church history. If nothing more, this

---

Reprinted by permission of UNITED EVANGELICAL ACTION Magazine, official publication of the National Association of Evangelicals.

surely suggests at least that small groups are conducive to the reviving ministry of the Holy Spirit.

Today the church needs to rediscover what the early Christians found: (1) Small group meetings are something essential to Christian experience and growth. (2) The success of a church function is not measured by body count. (3) Without the small group, the church in urban society simply does not experience one of the most basic essentials of the gospel—true, rich, deep, Christian fellowship or *koinonia*.

ADVANTAGES OF SMALL GROUP STRUCTURE

The small group offers a number of advantages over other forms of the church in a secular-urban world:

1. It is flexible.

Because the group is small, it can easily change its procedures or functions to meet changing situations or to accomplish different objectives. Because of its informality it has little need for rigid patterns of operation. It is *free to be flexible* as to the place, time, frequency, and length of its meetings. It can easily disband when it has fulfilled its purpose. These things can be said of virtually no other aspect of most church programming.

2. It is mobile.

A small group may meet in home, office, shop, or nearly any other place. It is not bound to that building on the corner of First and Elm that we call "church." It can go where the people are and doesn't have to rely on persuading strangers to enter a foreign environment.

3. It is inclusive.

The small group can demonstrate a winsome openness to people of all kinds. As Elton Trueblood says,

> When a person is drawn into a little circle, devoted to prayer and to deep sharing of spiritual resources, he is well aware that he is welcomed for his own sake, since the small group has no budget, no officers concerned with the success of their administration, and nothing to promote *(The Incendiary Fellowship,* p. 70).

The group provides the context in which a person can be seen, as Oswald Chambers put it, "as a fact, not as an illustration of a prejudice." Thus it holds some hope for overcoming social and racial barriers.

4. *It is personal.*

Christian communication suffers from impersonality. Often it is too slick, too professional—and therefore too impersonal. But in the small group, person meets person; communication takes place at the personal level. This is why, contradictory as it may seem, the small group may really reach more people than the mass communication media. The mass media reach millions superficially but few profoundly. The church should use all available forms of communication, but in proclaiming a personal Christ nothing can substitute for personal communication. The small group communicates on a personal basis. And even though small:

5. *It can grow by division.*

A small group is effective only while small, but it can easily reproduce itself by division. It can multiply into two, four, eight, or more, depending on the vitality of each group. There are endless possibilities for numerical growth without corresponding large financial outlays.

6. *It can be an effective means of evangelism.*

The evangelism which will be most effective in the city will use small groups as basic methodology. It will find that the small group provides the best environment in which sinners can hear the convicting, winning voice of the Holy Spirit and come alive spiritually through faith. It will find that *faith is contagious when fellowship is genuine.*

7. *It requires a minimum of professional leadership.*

Many laymen (and women) who could never direct a choir, preach a sermon, lead a youth group, or do house-to-house visitation could lead a small, home Bible study group. Competent lay leadership is needed in such groups, but experience has shown that such leaders can be developed in the average church through one or two key initial groups. A large staff of trained professionals is not required.

8. *It is adaptable to the institutional church*

The small group doesn't require throwing out the church. Small groups can be introduced without by-passing or undercutting the church—although the serious incorporation of small groups into the over-all ministry of the church requires some adjustments and inevitably raises some questions about priorities. The small group is best seen as an essential component of the church's structure and ministry, not as a replacement for the church.

Jess Moody says, "We will win the world when we realize that fellowship, not evangelism, must be our primary emphasis. When we demonstrate the Big Miracle of Love, it won't be necessary for us to go out—they will come in" (*A Drink at Joel's Place,* p. 24). I would say rather, our emphasis should be evangelism, *through* fellowship—and especially through small *koinonia* groups. That is coupling love's miracle with Christ's invitation.

It is questionable whether the institutional church can have a significant evangelistic ministry today through traditional methods. It may be able to build a denomination and carry out programs, but it will never turn the world rightside up. Most of today's methods are too big, too slow, too organized, too inflexible, too expensive and too professional to ever be truly dynamic in fast-faced urban society. If the contemporary church would shake loose from plant and program, from institutionalism and inflexibility, and would return to the dynamic of the early church, it must seriously and self-consciously build its ministry around the small group as basic structure.

THE PLACE OF THE SMALL GROUP IN CHURCH STRUCTURE

Three most helpful books on the proper place of small groups in the church are Robert A. Raines' *New Life in the Church* (Harper and Row, 1961) and George W. Webber's two books, *God's Colony in Man's World* and *The Congregation in Mission* (Abingdon, 1960, 1964).

Webber's books are especially significant because he is one of the very few who see the small group as *basic church structure*. Out of several years' experience in the early days of East Harlem Protestant Parish, Webber convincingly presents the case for the small group as the basic unit in the life of the congregation. He points out clearly that the small group is not merely another method—it is something more basic. His analysis is further relevant because it grows out of experience in an urban, inner-city setting—in a sense, a laboratory for the future.

I feel Webber's insights and experiences are so significant that they deserve some repeating here.

Webber writes,

> A new structure of congregational life is called for which makes provision for genuine meeting between persons, a context in which the masks of self-deception and distrust will be maintained only with difficulty and in which men and women will begin to relate to each other at the level of their true humanity in Christ *(The Congregation in Mission,* p. 121).

Each local church, therefore, should "make basic provision for its members to meet in small groups, not as a sidelight or an option for those who like it, but as a normative part of its life" *(Ibid.)*

Why? In part, because of modern patterns of living. In small-town America, and even in urban America in the past, Christians often lived close together in stable communities. But urbanization and technology have changed such patterns, not only in America but in many parts of the world. Modern technopolis in a different world. Thanks in part to urban mobility, we live in several distinct worlds in the course of a week—office, shop, neighborhood, school, club. The church is only one world among others. Thus today "we do not live in natural, human communities where we know each other in Christ and where, during the week, we have a chance to consider the implications of our faith together. *This must be built into the very structure of the life of the congregation."* (*God's Colony in Man's World,* pp. 58-59. Italics added.)

True, the church often brings believers together at other times than Sunday—but usually only the pious few, and then not in a way that encourages *koinonia.* The average church has no normative structure for true sharing and fellowship.

The small group, then, must be both supplemental and normative. Supplemental in that it does not replace corporate worship experiences. Normative in the sense of being basic church structure, equally important with corporate worship.

According to Acts 2:46 the early Christians spent their time "attending the temple together and breaking bread in their homes." "These are the two foci of our life as Christians about which I am speaking," says Webber. "We join in congregational worship. We meet in small groups" *(Ibid.).*

GROUPS EXIST FOR SERVICE

But the mere existence of small groups is not enough. Their function must be clearly understood. Their purpose is objective, not subjective. If the focus is subjectively on personal spiritual growth the groups turn inward and become self-defeating—like regularly pulling up the roots of a plant to see if it is growing. Rather the purpose of such groups "must be defined in objective terms that involve work to be done and goals to be achieved" *(Ibid.,* 122). They exist for service; they are "enabling groups" for Christian obedience in the world.

For the purpose of obedience and service, the small groups set before themselves the objective task of serious Bible study. The crucial fact is that something happens in Bible study in a small group that does not happen elsewhere. The Holy Spirit gives the unique gift of *koinonia* which makes

Bible study come alive. Thus Webber has discovered,

> People who have listened politely to sermons for years, when they gather together to listen to God's word from the Bible, are more likely to squirm in the face of honest confrontation, and only with difficulty can they brush aside the demands upon their lives *(Ibid.,* p. 82).

This awakening may not happen immediately, however. Webber and other writers have noted that weeks or months may pass before miracles happen. Says Robert Coleman, "The members must be honest with God and with each other. It may take a while to come to this freedom and trust. After all, you are not prone to bare your soul to people that you do not know" *(Dry Bones Can Live Again,* p. 70). Partially for this reason the small group must be essentially church structure, not merely a tentative experiment.

CONCLUSION

The small group can become basic structure in the local church if there is the vision for it and the will to innovate. The change probably cannot come without some rethinking of traditional programs, however. The midweek prayer meeting may have to go in favor of a number of midweek small group meetings, so the small groups don't take up another weeknight or become something merely tacked on. Other traditional services and activities may be replaced by small group meetings. In fact, the whole organization of the church's life may require review.

True, the small group is not a panacea. No effort of man can bring the church to greater faithfulness in meeting the needs and problems of the day except as the Holy Spirit directs and infills. But the small group is an essential component of the church's structure and life. In order for men to be moved upon by the Holy Spirit there must be openness toward God and toward others, an openness which best develops in a context of the supporting love and fellowship of other sincere seekers after God.

In the early days of the great Wesleyan Revival in England 200 years ago, John Wesley discovered the importance of the small group for his day. He instituted small cell groups—"class meetings"—for the conservation of converts. He soon found significant results. In reply to criticism of the method he wrote,

> Many now happily experienced that Christian fellowship of which they had not so much as an idea before. They began to "bear one another's burdens," and naturally to "care for each other." As they had daily a more intimate acquaintance with, so they had a more endeared affection for, each other ("A Plain Account of The People Called Methodists," *Works*, Zondervan Edition, VIII, p. 254).

In short, the early Methodists discovered the *koinonia* of the Holy Spirit through the use of small groups. Nothing was more characteristic of the Methodist revival than the class meeting of a dozen or so persons meeting together in private homes.

The Bible does not prescribe any particular pattern of church organization. But the practical necessities of our day suggest the need for small groups as basic to church structure.

CHAPTER 15

HOW TO EQUIP THE SAINTS FOR GOD'S SERVICE
OTIS E. YOUNG

FOR SOME TIME, I have been concerned about the church and the job that needs to be done in equipping all of us for ministry and service in the world as the people of God. Along with this, I have been concerned about the church helping persons to task and answer the deep questions of life and to be of help to them in meeting these questions head on. Also, I have been concerned that we offer to persons an opportunity to experience the joy and power which come as a result of Christians meeting together in an open and accepting atmosphere where deep personal concerns and problems can be shared with one another.

And then, since coming to my present pastorate, a number of my parishioners had spoken to me about becoming involved in a new and creative kind of group where persons could come together regularly to seek, to ask, and answer some of the deepest questions of life—questions such as, "What am I living for?" "What is the purpose of life?" "What is the goal of my life?" "What are the goals in our marriage?" "Who am I?" "Do I really know myself?" "Who is my neighbor?" "Who or what is God?" "How can I find meaning in my life?" The questions are almost endless.

Thus, after much thought and study, I sent an invitation to the members and friends of this congregation, inviting any interested persons who might want to participate in this unique endeavor to come to the parsonage on a Sunday night. I explained in the invitation and in our newsletter that we would explore the possibilities of starting a new kind of group, and I pointed out that the purpose would be nothing less than a complete reorientation to all of life.

It was my hope that through the group process, we would find a new basis for our living in today's world, plus a new awareness of living with ourselves and with others and, at the same time, learning to be sensitive to the needs of others, so that we would be equipped to minister to each other and to the world in a relevant way. It was, furthermore, my hope that in the process we would come to experience God's power and presence in our lives and in the life of the world in a fresh way, that we would find a new commitment to Jesus Christ, and know what the commitment entailed. Thus, in the invitation, I added the following phrase which was underlined, *"If you do not want to change, then do not consider becoming a part of such a group."* In the opening statement of the invitation I had also said, *"This may be the most important letter you have ever received."*

That Sunday night, forty-five interested persons came to the parsonage. This initial response was beyond my wildest expectations. We spent the evening discussing the project, and I outlined in detail what I had in mind. After much discussion and many questions, I invited those who were still interested to sign a sheet and to be prepared to commit themselves to come to a group meeting once a week for a period of one year. I stated that anyone who signed up for such a group would be expected to keep this discipline. Attendance at the group meetings was to be put first in our lives. Furthermore, there would be assignments made each week, and participants in the group would be expected to carry out each assignment to the best of their ability.

After setting out these requirements, I wondered if anyone was going to have courage enough to make the commitment. Well, that night and in the days following, enough persons signed up to form three groups, but because of scheduling, we had to combine into two groups. In the first group meeting on Sunday nights, ten couples agreed to the discipline and in the second group meeting on Monday nights, eight couples accepted—a total of thirty-six persons out of the forty-five who had come to the parsonage. Furthermore, several of the couples, who did not sign up, said they would like to join such a group in the fall. This was again beyond my wildest expectations. I told all of the people that I felt both groups were really too large, but we could talk no one into not coming. Since the beginning, we have had almost 100% in attendance at each meeting.

Now briefly, what happens in our weekly gatherings? We meet in each other's homes and begin at approximately 8:30 p.m. The atmosphere is informal and relaxed. As we arrive, coffee is ready and most of us get a cup and then visit for a few minutes. There is usually much laughter and fun.

Then we settle down to business for the discussion which usually goes on until about 10:30 or 11:00 p.m. I mentioned earlier that each week an assignment is made to the members of the group. These assignments are not something to be read, but rather are an experiment to be carried out in the individual's or couple's life. Thus, the first part of the discussion each evening is a kind of sharing and reporting to each other concerning the results or lack of results in the assigned experiments. Then later in the evening, the discussion is opened completely so that any one can share anything he has on his mind. There is a complete openness and freedom. Here a person can truly be himself. We are not trying to impress each other, but rather to accept and love each other as we are, simply because we are persons, children of God. In this sense, we minister to each other in the deepest ways. Here is the church truly in action. Here is the ministry of the laity.

The over-all outline of the experiments and assignments for those participating in the groups is based on the great commandment. Love God, and love your neighbor as yourself. However, in order to love God and our neighbor and in order to love ourselves, we need first of all to become aware of ourselves as individuals; we need to know ourselves better, to know who we are and what we stand for. We need to know our fears, our weaknesses, our failures, our sins, as well as our talents and our strengths.

Thus for the first twelve weeks, we had experiments assigned to us in order to help us know ourselves better, so that we would become more aware of ourselves as distinct individuals. The second area we are now engaged in is that of becoming more aware and sensitive of others and more aware of how much we really need others. Later on we will enter the third stage—that of becoming more aware of God as a power and force in our everyday lives, and how God works through us. All of these three areas of course overlap and are interrelated and dependent on one another. All are a part of the great commandment as stated by Jesus in the New Testament.

PRINCIPLES AND PURPOSES

But now let's look more specifically at some of the principles and purposes, at the theology behind such groups as these, and why such groups are necessary and vital to us as human beings and as Christians.

1. First of all, we believe that the basic human drive, the basic appetite, the basic deep down desire of all persons is not self-preservation—that is too much merely biological. The basic drive is not sex, not pleasure, or any of the other things we like to think. What man wants—every man and

woman on earth—is "meaning." All of us seek a reason for our living and working. We seek goals and we have goals. All of us want something that will give purpose and direction to our lives.

All of us seek to make sense out of life even without knowing it. The problem is that many of our reasons for living and working are inadequate in themselves, and eventually we discover that we have been serving a false god. For some of us now, for example, our major goal is to see that our children are raised properly, but one day our children will be gone and will have their own families. What then will be our reason for living? And so it goes. All of us, even though we are not aware of it, have certain goals and purposes we serve.

A woman said of her husband, "His way of life doesn't make sense." In private conversation, the man himself also said that his life didn't make sense. When he was asked why he worked so hard and was busy in so many community activities, he replied, "If I didn't do what I'm doing, I would lose my self-respect." Thus we observe that his way of life, far from being senseless, is his way of trying to find worth, his worth in the world, his reason for living. Even though the man said with words that his way of life didn't make sense, deep down, at the same time, he was working at trying to make some sense out of life.

All of us in similar ways seek meaning and worth in our living. We all seek a "why" for our living. And we all give answers implicitly all the time, and many times without even knowing it, just as we find short-term reasons for working and living. But we all need to discover a deeper, more basic meaning in our lives and we can do this only by talking with significant others—by sharing with them our deepest ideas, our deepest fears, our strongest doubts. We need to seek, together, meaning in life. We can never find the true answer to our basic desires by ourselves.

OVERCOMING SEPARATION

2. Secondly, we believe that a person's meaning and purpose in life comes primarily from his relationship with his fellows. In relationship, if it is vital, is purpose, the "why" for living. To put it in a negative way, a person's life begins to lose meaning, purpose, and direction most rapidly when he becomes estranged from his fellows. To put it another way, the deepest desire of all of us is to be at one with someone, to have someone who can be at one with us, and through whom we can find at-one-ness with all.

All of our life, therefore, is an effort to overcome our separation and to find each other in fulfilling relationships, and this includes our relationship with God.

We seek in many ways to overcome our separations. Many seek to overcome the pain of loneliness that grows out of separation by their membership in organizations—civic, fraternal, social, and religious, each time hoping to find people with whom they can be close; people with whom they will be accepted as they are. Many come to the church hoping for the same thing. However, the sad fact is that in our time man does not often find his deepest needs satisfied in our usual institutional structures, including the church as we know it.

Another way in which people try to overcome their separation from others and therefore from God can be seen in the way they seek out anyone who will listen to them when they need to talk. And if the listeners have ears to hear, they hear people talking mostly about their loneliness and their sense of separation. This is one reason why counselors are in such great demand. A sign of the state of alienation in which we live is seen in the fact that only by paying someone to listen can some of us find people who will listen to us.

The point is that we all need the kind of encounters and relationships in which each gives the other the freedom to be, in which each gives the other acceptance and understanding. And the significance of this kind of relationship is that it is just as important to be able to give as it is to receive.

But the problem is further compounded in that many times we are so preoccupied with our own needs and have little or nothing to spare from our neighbors, that we turn away from each other, thus making our situation worse than before.

All of this is why reconciliation is such a big word in the Christian faith. Because of our loneliness and anxiety resulting from separation and alienation from ourselves, each other, and God, we want someone with whom we can be at one, who can be at one with us, and through whom we can find at-one-ness with all. This is the deepest want of all of us, and the fact of our need is not at all dependent upon our being aware of it. All of us are moved by this desire whether we know it or not, and in one way or another we are seeking such at-one-ness—many of us in the wrong way or in ways that are not long satisfying.

We believe and have experienced the fact that in relation to this need for at-one-ness the Gospel of Jesus Christ is the good news. God came to us in a person in answer to man's need. We are discovering in our groups that God in Christ speaks to persons through persons seeking to accomplish his purpose in us and through us. "God's purpose is such, and he so made humanity in accordance with that purpose, that he never enters into personal relationship with a man apart from other human persons." (H. H. Farmer)

Since we were made for relationship with God and with one another, the hurt of alienation remains unhealed until touched by the healing of a new, and this time, accepting relationship. Thus a new kind of group is needed in the church. We believe that we are finding new meaning and purpose in our living and that we are experiencing God's reconciliation in and through our relationships with one another in these groups. And because of the relationship with those in the groups, we are also finding our relationship with others outside the group more exciting and meaningful. (For a fuller treatment of these ideas, see *Man's Need and God's Action,* by Reuel Howe.)

MEANING AND HEALTH

3. Thirdly, we believe that man's overall health and well-being is involved here. There is now increasing scientific and medical evidence that man's physical and psychological health are profoundly affected by the degree to which he has found meaning, direction, and purpose in his existence, and to the degree that he has overcome the separation between himself and his fellow man.

Victor Frankl tells us in his book, *From Death Camp to Existentialism,* that the inmates in the prison camp who could find meaning in their suffering and who had a purpose for living survived incredible stress, while others died.

In the matter of illnesses of all kinds, it has now been shown that people become more susceptible to an infection when they are hopeless, without direction. We've discussed this fact a great deal in our groups and have discovered that most of us get colds and other infections almost always after some letdown in our lives, and most often this is associated with some kind of alienation among those in our family or most intimate friends.

One study which I recently read shows that almost all the patients admitted to a general hospital with organic illness during a one-month period had sustained some emotional crisis involving loss of meaning and purpose, which incidentally almost always involved a breakdown in the human relationships which surrounded their lives. This had always happened shortly before the onset of the illness.

Dr. Paul Tournier in his book, *The Healing of Persons,* shows this fact to be true over and over again, and he cites case history after case history to illustrate the point. It has been estimated that except for perhaps 15% of all illness, physical and mental, rest or change and restored human relationships, finding new meaning in life, will permit the body to restore itself. The problem is that official medicine and mass media have not sufficiently publicized the healing power of changed conduct and restored human relationships, but seem to place more faith in the healing power of drugs.

DISCLOSING OURSELVES TO OTHERS

4. Fourthly, we believe that in order to have a true and productive relationship with others, one must come to know himself, and the plain fact is that we come to know ourselves only as we disclose ourselves to significant others, and this means more than just one other person.

To put it another way, no man can know himself except as the outcome of disclosing himself to others. When we disclose ourselves to others in an accepting, loving group, we come to see ourselves as in a mirror—the process of telling and revealing helps us to understand who we are and what we think and feel. We may have thought we knew before, but we didn't. In our groups we are coming to know ourselves in a new way as we disclose ourselves to others, and the experiments are so designed that they help us to do this. In the process, our lives are being changed.

I remember one night, as we were sharing our feelings, when one of the group members began telling us her feelings about the schools her children had attended and the problems it seemed to cause. She was quite critical of much that had happened. And then when she finished, she said very candidly, "You know, I didn't know I felt that way about the schools." She was coming to know herself in the process of disclosing herself to others. This has happened to all of us over and over again.

Most people, I fear, have usually chosen to conceal their authentic being behind various masks. We conceal and camouflage our true being before others to foster a sense of safety, to protect ourselves against unwanted but expected criticism, hurt, or rejection. We are afraid of truly knowing ourselves or of letting others truly know us. This protection is purchased at a steep price. When we are not truly known by others in our lives, we are misunderstood and we misunderstand ourselves and others. We are not aware then of the forces operating within us which make us act as we do. Thus, we are really slaves to forces we do not understand and we are not free to love or to be loved.

And then, worse still, when we succeed in hiding ourselves from others, we tend not only to lose touch with our real selves, but this loss of self makes it more and more difficult to relate to others, and this, together with a loss of meaning in our living, contributes to both physical and mental illness in its myriad forms.

To sum up, we believe that our Christian faith shows us and continually reminds us that man is a social animal—that we are made for each other and need each other. Furthermore, without true and deep communication with others we die, if not physically, then spiritually and mentally.

This is true even of the tiniest baby. Perhaps you have heard of an experiment carried on many years ago. The Emperor Frederick determined to isolate infants from the moment of their birth so that they would never hear human speech. He thought in this way he would discover the original language of mankind. To accomplish this, he arranged for wet nurses to raise the babies—the nurses he instructed to maintain absolute silence. The nurses succeeded. According to the account, not one of them uttered a single word to any of the children. But the children all died. What was true for the children is true for us. We need others in order to live. We need them in every level of relationship. We need communication with one another.

In our research groups we are discovering just how important communication—more than just superficial communication—is with one another as we share our problems, our joys, and our sorrows and sins. We are finding a new freedom to be ourselves. We have found it to be true, as one man wrote, "The crucial element in mental health and in our lives as a whole, is the degree of openness and communion which a person has with his fellow men. This more than anything determines whether we as persons will prosper or perish. Man was made for fellowship and when he violates his human connectedness, he dies." To put it another way, sin is our assertion that we are sufficient of ourselves and that we do not need relationship with God and man.

Man is an individual, distinct and unique and, at the same time, he is a social being who needs others. Movements like Communism forget individuality, and movements at the other extreme forget man's social needs. Christianity affirms both. Thus every person needs a group where he can be himself as a distinct individual and be accepted in his uniqueness, including his failures and his successes, and at the same time the group needs to give him what he needs as a social being—the communion and fellowship without which we perish. This is certainly, in the highest sense, some of what the church is meant to be.

ABOUT THE AUTHORS

C. S. Lewis has been called one of this century's ablest defenders of the Christian faith because of the power and clarity of books like *Mere Christianity, Miracles* and *The Problem of Pain*. He was also known for his adult fantasy (*Perelandra*) and his children's stories (*The Chronicles of Narnia*).

George Sweeting, president of the Moody Bible Institute, has traveled extensively as an evangelist, and is a well-known lecturer and author.

Frederic Hood was a noted clergyman in the Church of England famed for direct and lucid talks and writing. He was particularly concerned with elucidating the divine scheme for mankind as set forth in Christ's teachings, and the practical life of the Church on earth.

J. I. Packer taught at Tyndale Hall and was warden of Latimer House, Oxford, before becoming associate principal of Trinity College, Bristol, England. His *Knowing God* and *Fundamentalism and the Word of God* have gone through many printings.

Claude H. Thompson is a professor at Candler School of Theology, Emory University. He received his Ph.D. from Drew Theological Seminary and spent a year studying under the Pilling Fellowship in Systematic Theology.

About the Authors

Donald Fields, a graduate of Indiana University and Fuller Theological Seminary, has spent a number of years as an InterVarsity Christian Fellowship area director.

J. Oswald Sanders, principal of the Christian Leaders' Training College, New Guinea, has written many books in several different languages. Titles available in English include *Mighty Faith, Effective Prayer,* and *The Divine Art of Soul-Winning.*

Edith Schaeffer spends much of her time ministering with her husband, Francis, at L'Abri, a Christian retreat center in Switzerland. She has written five books and has a regular column in CHRISTIANITY TODAY.

Charles Ryrie, currently dean of doctoral studies and professor of systematic theology at Dallas Theological Seminary has written widely on the Bible and Christian faith.

Bob Sheffield is Midwest regional director of the Navigators.

Elisabeth Elliot has written nine books, the most recent entitled *These Strange Ashes.* Twice widowed, she is well acquainted with both the suffering and hope that death brings to the Christian.

Robert Webber is associate professor of Bible at Wheaton College. He has written extensively on issues facing evangelical Christians. He is currently at work on a major project evaluating the basis of the evangelical faith.

L. Nelson Bell, father-in-law of Billy Graham, served as a medical missionary in China for 25 years. He was a founder and executive editor of CHRISTIANITY TODAY, and a director of the Billy Graham Evangelistic association until his death in 1973.

About The Authors

Howard A. Snyder, formerly dean of the Free Methodist Theological Seminary in Sao Paulo, Brazil, is currently executive director of Light and Life Men International. He was a major speaker at the International Congress on World Evangelization in Lausanne, Switzerland. His book, *The Problem of Wineskins,* has recently been published.

Otis E. Young is pastor of the Evangelical United Church of Christ, Webster Groves, Missouri.

Jan P. Dennis, editor of this volume, has written for a number of Christian and secular periodicals. Formerly with the American Bible Society, he holds the master of English literature degree and is currently working in Christian printing and publishing.